JANE HARRISON is descended from the Muruwari people of NSW. Her first play, *Stolen*, had productions across Australia and toured internationally. She was co-winner of the 2012 RAKA Kate Challis Award for *Stolen*. *Rainbow's End* has had numerous productions since its premiere in 2003 and won the 2012 Drovers Award for best touring production. Both *Stolen* and *Rainbow's End* have been placed on secondary school curricula. *The Visitors* premiered at Sydney Festival in 2020. Her novel *Becoming Kirrali Lewis* won the 2014 Black & Write! Prize, and was shortlisted for the Prime Minister's Literary Awards and the Victorian Premier's Literary Awards.

Jane believes that stories have the power to reframe our national identity.

Kerri Simpson (left) as Lawrence and John Blair as Jacob in the Sydney Festival/Moogahlin Performing Arts/Carriageworks production in 2020. (Photo: Jamie James)

THE VISITORS

Jane Harrison

CURRENCY PRESS
The performing arts publisher

CURRENCY PLAYS

First published in 2021
by Currency Press Pty Ltd,
PO Box 2287, Strawberry Hills, NSW, 2012, Australia
enquiries@currency.com.au
www.currency.com.au

Typeset by Dean Nottle for Currency Press.
Cover image: Daniel Boyd, *Untitled (FF)*, 2017, oil and archival glue on linen, 193.5 x 302 cm. Photo: Jessica Maurer. Courtesy of the artist and Roslyn Oxley9 Gallery, Sydney.
Cover design by Emma Bennetts for Currency Press.

Currency Press acknowledges the Traditional Owners of the Country on which we live and work. We pay our respects to all Aboriginal and Torres Strait Islander Elders, past and present.

NATIONAL LIBRARY OF AUSTRALIA
A catalogue record for this book is available from the National Library of Australia

Contents

In accordance with the requirement of the Australian Media, Entertainment and Arts Alliance, Currency Press has made every effort to identify, and gain the permission of, the artists who appear in the photographs that illustrate this play.

Kerri Simpson (left) as Lawrence and Leroy Parsons as Walter in the Sydney Festival/Moogahlin Performing Arts/Carriageworks production in 2020. (Photo: Jamie James)

INTRODUCTION

Australia has a messed-up sense of history. As a country based on the legal fiction of Terra Nullius, Australia has found it difficult to tell accurate histories about its colonial past. Stories of massacres, dispossession, attempts at cultural eradication and much more have either gone untold, supressed or denied. Anthropologist William Stanner, in his 1968 Boyer Lecture called 'After the Dreaming', talked of the Great Australian Silence, and a vested interest in forgetting the past to avoid the truth of history. Fifty years later, Rachel Perkins, in her Boyer Lecture entitled 'The End of Silence', talked of the power of truth-telling to help blaze a path forward, the role of a constitutionally recognised voice for First Nations Australians and the freedoms that would come for all Australians when we embraced the fullness of our whole history of occupation of this continent.

In 1995, newly elected South African President Nelson Mandela established a Truth and Reconciliation Commission as a way of bringing restorative justice to a country that had seen untold number of horrors in the name of Apartheid. The history was complex and divisive with a great deal of contentious and conflicting narratives. As part of the process of truth-telling, the TRC helped shape a definition of truth that was inclusive and empowering to allow all aggrieved parties to speak. The TRC adopted a four-part recognition of Truth:

- Personal Truth—the truth that an individual or group understood as the truth;
- Official Truth—the truth recognised and recorded in the public records, media et cetera.;
- Forensic Truth—the truth that could be proven through a scientific evidence-based lens;
- Healing or Community Truth—the truth that all could accept and come together on.

It is interesting to reflect that in 1991, in response to a recommendation of the Royal Commission into Aboriginal Deaths in Custody, Australia established a Council for Aboriginal Reconciliation that would have a life span of ten years. Its purpose was written into the legislation, reading:

> The object of the establishment of the Council is to promote a process of reconciliation between Aborigines and Torres Strait Islanders and the wider Australian community, based on an appreciation by the Australian community as a whole of Aboriginal and Torres Strait Islander cultures and achievements and of the unique position of Aborigines and Torres Strait Islanders as the indigenous peoples of Australia, and by means that include the fostering of an ongoing national commitment to co-operate to address Aboriginal and Torres Strait Islander disadvantage.[i]

The telling of hard histories is implied in this statement but stops short of embracing a whole truth-telling process, instead focussing on reconciliation first and foremost. Truth-telling has become the rallying cry of the Australian modern era and like the definitions used in South Africa it has become important to see truth as a function of perspective and often dominated by self-serving narratives restating colonial imperatives.

In a year that could only be described as an absolute dumpster fire, 2020 was to mark the 250th anniversary of the voyage of the *Endeavour* captained by Lieutenant James Cook. Bushfires and Covid-19 meant the suspension of the planned re-enactments and other events but, before this welcome demise, the debate raged about the role of memory-making and memorials. While the USA was dealing with its own Trump-inspired sense of disconnection from truth and evidence, and race relations hit another disastrous low point, the role of statues and memorials was raised in Australia. What is the role of a statue to James Cook in the truth-telling of Australia? In 2017, in response to the tearing down of statues and monuments marking USA Confederate leaders and racist events, broadcaster and commentator Stan Grant dared to question the role of the narrative that Captain Cook 'discovered' Australia. It was with great interest that I observed the pile-on by a bevy of conservative commentators and politicians. As Stan Grant wrote in August 2017:

> Who would have thought the mere suggestion that Captain Cook did not in fact discover Australia would be so controversial? It seems to have taken some people by surprise, the idea that people were here for more than 60,000 years before the *Endeavour* dropped anchor. What were we doing all that time, just waiting for white people to find us?[ii]

He goes on to talk about history being a 'hymn to whiteness', a 'damaging myth', and the fact that history is a process of writing in and out of the stories we choose, that history is a choice that highlights and makes silent the events and people who have left a mark on the past. Captain Cook is not just a person, Captain Cook is a narrative we have chosen to help write out the millennia of Blak history and to reinforce the narratives of Terra Nullius, white superiority and the righteous colonial and modern occupation of the continent. So it is with January 26, 1788.

Eighteen years after the *Endeavour* crew mapped the eastern coastline of Australia and eventually raised a flag claiming it for the British Empire, the First Fleet arrived in Botany Bay on January 19 and 20, 1788 to find that Cook's records were not as truthful as they were led to believe, with poor soil, a lack of fresh water and the harbour not deep enough to anchor close to shore.[iii] And so the First Fleet under the command of Arthur Phillip moved to Port Jackson (later Sydney Cove) arriving on January 26, 1788.

The two events of the voyage of the *Endeavour* and the arrival of the First Fleet get confused all the time. The claiming of the continent and the raising of the British flag we have all come to associate with Sydney Cove was first done on an island named Bedanug in the Torres Strait. Cook named it Possession Island, but this was done on August 22, 1770—over three months after the week spent in Kamay, which they named Botany Bay. Because very few people know the relevant dates concerning the voyage of the *Endeavour* (April 29, 1770—arrival at Kamay; June 10, 1770—ran aground and was shipwrecked in Gooreng Gooreng country for six weeks; August 22, 1770—landing at Bedanug), January 26 has often become the repository of the all the foundation narratives of our country. A survey from 2017 stated:

> One-in-five Australians claimed Australia Day marked Captain Cook's discovery of Australia, while one-in-six said it was the anniversary of Australia's Federation. A small proportion said the date commemorated an important battle in World War I.[iv]

This highlights the intersection of the 'discovery', colonisation, country-forming and ANZAC narratives as they get apportioned to a single day in our calendar and how little knowledge those surveyed had about January 26. I argue there is vested interest in confusing and intertwining these narratives. The two events of the arrivals of the *Endeavour* and the First

Fleet become synonymous because they are crafted to act like the statue of Captain Cook, a statement of perspective and a permanent marker in time that argues legitimacy and power. Megan Davies talks about each Australia Day becoming more toxic as the gap between the rhetoric of the day and the anniversary it marks clashes with the aspirations of the nation and its people to find a more encompassing storytelling and action.[v]

Who gets to name a place? Why is there so much confusion around the foundation narratives of this country? What role do First Nations Australians play in the storytelling of this country?

The predominant histories of this country have been written by those with an interest in solidifying their dominance and ownership of this continent. Given the oral storytelling nature of Indigenous Australian cultures, it is no surprise that our narratives have been closely held and protected during the onslaught of the colonial project. Stories and language, cultural knowledges and practices have been passed down and shared around the campfires away from the heavy disapproving hand of the coloniser and it is no accident that storytelling in the form of theatre, film, song, dance and art-making have been where we have found strength and power in the modern era.

Jane Harrison is a playwright who has built her reputation on writing on to the public record our narrative from our perspective. From her works *Stolen* and *Rainbow's End* you see a strong combination of social justice, role modelling, historical reframing and an antidote to the oppressive anthropology of the white gaze. *The Visitors* takes as its starting point the view from the shore as the First Fleet arrive through Sydney Heads and asks the question: what did we think when these ships came eighteen years after Cook fired the first shots at the Eora? Harrison follows in the footsteps of '80s classics 'Basically Black' and *BabaKiueria* by shifting the framing of the conversation and recasting the dominant point of view to reflect our way of seeing the world. She does this not by alienating the audience but by drawing them in through familiar constructions of debate and discussion, she stipulates the gathered council wear suits to show status, they speak English to invite understanding, and express cultural perspectives throughout to demonstrate a First Nations view of this foundation event.

Harrison brings wit and charm through the debate like a gathering of jurors sifting through evidence to arrive at agreement. There is not one viewpoint, there is not unanimous settlement, there is not a right or wrong. Drama works best when it can find voice for a diversity of arguments and allow an audience to decide.

Like many of Harrison's works, *The Visitors* took a long time to develop and to be produced. Some of the hesitation of producers to get on board with the storytelling I attribute to an inability to see the value in a First Nations perspective in the national narrative. The contention and debate around January 26 and Australia Day I think scared off the white conservative elements of our theatre-making community and demonstrates a lack of imagination and negation of the role of storytelling to contribute to the redefinition of what this country could be. When this show, produced by Moogahlin Performing Arts, sold out during the 2020 Sydney Festival and extra performances had to be scheduled to fulfil demand, you got the sense that these fears were unfounded. Australians are in search of new meaning for old colonial relics and to place these abandoned and confused foundation narratives more in relation to the 60,000-plus years of human occupation of this continent.

We need more plays like *The Visitors* to help shape the future by relooking at history through a more informed and educated point of view.

Wesley Enoch
December 2020

Wesley Enoch is a writer and director for the stage. He was the Artistic Director of Queensland Theatre Company from 2010 to 2015 and is the current Artistic Director at the Sydney Festival. He hails from Stradbroke Island (Minjeribah) and is a proud Noonuccal Nuugi man.

i https://www.legislation.gov.au/Details/C2004C03090

ii https://www.abc.net.au/news/2017-08-23/stan-grant:-damaging-myth-captain-cook-discovered-australia/8833536

iii Derek Parker: Arthur Phillip: Australia's First Governor, Woodslane Press, Sydney 2009.

iv https://www.sbs.com.au/news/survey-reveals-most-australians-don-t-know-what-australia-day-is-for

v https://www.griffithreview.com/articles/long-road-uluru-walking-together-truth-before-justice-megan-davis/

From left: Glenn Shea as Joseph, Kerri Simpson as Lawrence, John Blair as Jacob, Damion Hunter as Gordon, Colin Kinchela as Albert, Nathan Leslie as Gary, and Leroy Parsons as Walter in the Sydney Festival/Moogahlin Performing Arts/Carriageworks production in 2020.
(Photo: Jamie James)

ACKNOWLEDGEMENTS

My first responsibility is back to my community, and while there is no one 'community', I have been blessed with support from many First Nations individuals and companies whilst developing this script. I am aware of the sensitivity in me, as a First Nations woman, telling a 'men's' story and mostly I was encouraged by the many First Nations men who were involved, so a huge thankyou to the fellas.

The idea for this play had been percolating for many years before Maryrose Casey invited me to be writer-in-residence at the Monash University Indigenous Studies Centre. There, I put down a complete first draft, with a script reading culminating the residency. My two cultural consultants during the residency were Tony Birch and Robyne Latham. I am most grateful.

Across its many years of development, various organisations provided support in many forms—time, workshopping, feedback, audiences and funding including: Ilbijerri Theatre Company, Monash University, Moogahlin Performing Arts (Yellamundie Festival), Playwriting Australia, Melbourne Theatre Company, Cybec Electric, Melbourne Indigenous Arts Festival, the Victorian College of the Arts and the Australia Council for the Arts. A huge thankyou.

Waving the dramaturgical wand at various times was the adored Aiden Fennessey, Francesca Smith, Chris Mead and Fred Copperwaite. I've had the incredible privilege to work with directors Glenn Shea, Leah Purcell, Wayne Blair and Fred Copperwaite.

I am indebted to the many superb actors who have contributed to the play's development: Glenn Shea, Greg Fryer, along with a number of theatre students from Monash University (sorry, I have no record of your names), James Henry, Aaron Pederson, Wayne Blair, Leroy Parsons, Sermsah Bin Saad, Kamahi Djordan King, Glenn Maynard, Troy Russell, Robert Preston, John Blair, Damion Hunter, Jason De Santis, Kirk Page, Robert Preston, Shane Bell and Sonny Dallas Law.

The Visitors premiered at the 2020 Sydney Festival. The premiere was supported by Create NSW, Australia Council for the Arts, City of Sydney, the Seaborn, Broughton & Walford Foundation, and the Australian Government through the Department of Communications and the Arts and Catalyst—Australian Arts and Culture Fund. I particularly want to acknowledge the producers, Moogahlin Performing Arts. It was a big leap to stage a play of its size and scope. 'The Incredibles'—Lily Shearer, Liza-Mare Syron, Fred Copperwaite and Ali Murphy-Oates—made it happen. Thank you Fred Copperwaite, for your steady yet ambitious direction. To the cast: John Blair, Damion Hunter, Colin Kinchela, Nathan Leslie, Leroy Parsons, Glenn Shea, and Kerri Simpson, my gratitude for your powerful and moving performances. Thank you to the set, sound, lighting designers and crew, and all of those working behind the scenes to make the magic happen on the night.

Sydney Festival Artistic Director Wesley Enoch deserves a big mob of credit for his encouragement and sector leadership over many, many years. Much appreciation to Currency Press for our long-standing publishing relationship.

And for everything you do, and what you mean to me: my daughters Savannah and Nova, and my partner Dominic. Love, love, love.

Jane Harrison

The Visitors was first produced by Sydney Festival, Moogahlin Performing Arts and Carriageworks, on 22 January 2020, with the following cast:

JACOB	John Blair
GORDON	Damion Hunter
ALBERT	Colin Kinchela
GARY	Nathan Leslie
WALTER	Leroy Parsons
JOSEPH	Glenn Shea
LAWRENCE	Kerri Simpson

Director, Frederick Copperwaite
Set and Costume Design, Lisa Mimmochi
Lighting Design, Chloe Ogilvie
Sound Design, Phil Downing, with additional composition from Tim Gray
Producer, Liza-Mare Syron
Assistant Producers, Corrine Shepherd and Sonny Dallas Law
Production Manager, Oliver Anstis
Stage Manager, Farlie Goodwin
Deputy Stage Manager, Meagan Fitzpatrick
Wardrobe Supervisor, Lissette Endacott
Set Construction, Hamish Elliott, Camille Ostrowsky and Matthew Hinton
Community Liaison, Tim Gray

The Visitors was developed with the assistance of Monash University Faculty of Arts, 2011, the Yellamundie Festival, 2013, and Moogahlin Performing Arts 2019.

The play was workshopped with the assistance of Playwriting Australia and Melbourne Theatre Company in 2013 and at Melbourne Theatre Company in 2016.

It was produced as part of the Cybec Electric playreading series, Melbourne Theatre Company, and Melbourne Indigenous Arts Festival in 2014.

Financial support was provided by an Australia Council Grant.

Damion Hunter (left) as Gordon and Colin Kinchela as Albert in the Sydney Festival/Moogahlin Performing Arts/Carriageworks production in 2020. (Photo: Jamie James)

CHARACTERS

GARY, Wallumedegal man, Northern Parramatta River mob. The 'Bureaucrat/Numbers Man'.

LAWRENCE, young Gweagal man, Botany Bay mob, Fire Clan. Youngest. 'Almost initiated'.

GORDON, Cadigal man, Sydney Cove–harbour-dwelling Clan. The 'General'.

ALBERT, Wangal man, South Shore Clan. The 'Engineer/Mr Logic'.

JACOB, Cameragal man, Manly Cove–North Shore Clan. The 'Joker'. The 'Tradie'.

WALTER, Burramattagal man, River mob. Eel Place Clan. The 'Anthropologist/Philosopher'.

JOSEPH, Kameygal, man Headlands of the Bay, Spear Clan, La Perouse area. The 'Doctor/Healer'.

SETTING

On an escarpment overlooking a harbour. Sandstone cliffs and bush.

CONVENTIONS

Seven Aboriginal Elders. Although it is 1788, they wear fine modern suits and the props are modern. They bring spears and shields with them.

— means an interruption.

▼ ▼ ▼ means a change—of mood, physical action, position relative to one another, soundscape or lighting—as the director sees fit.

It is January, the weather is stifling, the rare and unusual mammatus clouds spectacular. The sound of cicadas and birds and the sea.

A lone man, WALTER, *stands on the edge of an escarpment, looking out to sea (the audience). He is lost in thought. Although morning, it is blindingly hot. After a time,* GORDON *arrives. He is a big man, a warrior, fit.*

GORDON: Red sky at morning.

It isn't said directly to WALTER *but he doesn't acknowledge it anyway.*

GORDON *starts pacing, working out his action plan. He has to physicalise it, as words aren't his thing.*

After a time, JOSEPH *arrives quietly. He is meticulous. He pulls a kerchief from his chest pocket and pats his brow, folding the kerchief neatly back into the pocket.*

Welcome, Grandfather.

JOSEPH: Gordon. Respects to your country.

GORDON: Received. Decent trip?

JOSEPH: Decent. The ants were frenzied.

GORDON: Storm on its way.

Niceties over, JOSEPH *walks over to join* WALTER *while* GORDON *resumes pacing.* WALTER *silently embraces* JOSEPH. *There's no need for words between them.* JOSEPH *follows* WALTER*'s line of sight.*

JOSEPH: Did you ever imagine?

Again, WALTER *doesn't respond. After a time they hear crashing through the bush and* GORDON *stops pacing.*

Jacob.

JACOB *bursts onto the escarpment, swearing under his breath.*

GORDON: I could hear you three waves before you appeared. Remind me to never use you as a scout.

JACOB: Bros. I can be silent when required. Quiet as a bush mouse. But no need for subterfuge just for a meeting. Grandfather …

JOSEPH: Jacob.

JACOB *and* GORDON *do the blackfella handshake.*

JACOB: How you doing, big fella?
GORDON: Fighting fit, bros. You?
JACOB: Well, it took three sunrises to get here, overland—

GARY *has appeared.*

—due to this fella instructing me that I couldn't travel by water—
GARY: Just a precaution. [*To* GORDON] Respect to your country, Gordon.
GORDON: Welcome, Gary.
GARY: [*to* JACOB] Surprise is our best defence.
JACOB: Whatever. Just a pain going overland. When it would've been a short trip as the fish swim. Sunrise to mid sun by nowee.

GARY *looks out at sea.*

GARY: Speaking of which ... never in my lifetime have I witnessed that.
GORDON: Not for long.
GARY: Not for long.

GORDON *and* GARY *shake hands.* JACOB *and* GARY *shake hands.* JACOB *turns to* GORDON *while* GARY *is left standing alone.*

GORDON: How's the family?
JACOB: In great health. Expanding. Another little one on the way.
GORDON: Serious? Since last time?
JACOB: Haha. Grandfather reckons it's something in the water. I reckon it's something in my waters, aye. Your family?
GORDON: Solid. Young fellas getting stronger.
JACOB: We'll get to test 'em out today.
GORDON: They'll enjoy that.

GARY *has joined* JOSEPH *and they have exchanged greetings.*

GARY: Grandfather. You're looking well after such a long walk. Younger. Even in this heat.
JOSEPH: A parakeet fell from the sky, stone dead, and landed at my feet.
GARY: Strange times?
JOSEPH: Strange time. Perhaps that's Albert?

They listen.

Yes.

ALBERT *enters the escarpment.*

ALBERT: Respect to your country, Gordon. Ah, that view.
JACOB: Everyone loves a water view.
ALBERT: The view has been somewhat spoilt.
GARY: Speaking of which, the purpose of this meeting—
JACOB: We starting the formal stuff already? How about a feed first? We've all come a long way. 'Cept Gordo.
GORDON: Yeah, tuck in. Rock oysters, Goolwa cockles, pippis, red cockles, sand cockles. Collected this morning. Tuck in, fellas.

▼ ▼ ▼

They eat. WALTER *hasn't joined them.*

JOSEPH: Good tucker.
JACOB: The eel eater isn't joining us?

He indicates WALTER.

ALBERT: He's *contemplating*.

JACOB *grabs more food.*

JOSEPH: [*to* ALBERT] Albert, did you ever expect to see them back again? Those shiny ones?
ALBERT: They come. They go.
JACOB: Shiny ones?
JOSEPH: Under their cloaks they are. Shiny and pink. Like the inside of a shell.

JACOB *laughs.*

They finish eating, tossing their shells in a pile. The midden.

GARY: Okay then.
JACOB: Let's get on with it.

They move over to take their places in the circle.

GARY: Walter, would you mind joining us?

But WALTER *is still lost in thought.*

Walter? Brother?
JACOB: [*under his breath*] Tidda.
WALTER: Pardon me. I was contemplating.

ALBERT: Told ya.

A few laugh.

JACOB: [*under his breath*] Spare us.
JOSEPH: Your contemplation, sir?
WALTER: I was wondering … how we would remember this day.
JACOB: As a day we'll never get back.
ALBERT: For the excellent feed, thank you, Gordon.
JOSEPH: The ridiculous heat.
GARY: Before we start waxing lyrical, let's get through the meeting protocols.
JACOB: Highlight of my summer.
GARY: We speak one at a time, using the message stick. Agreed?
We listen more than we speak.
We stay until we all agree.
The agreement is for the greater good, not favouring any one clan group. Agreed?
ALL: Yes. Yep. Yes.
GARY: No gossip. Agreed?
ALL: Of course. Yes.
GARY: Lastly, have you given instructions that the women are not to approach them, nor the children?[1]
ALL: Yes.
JACOB: Hang on. How are the girls going to fish if they're not allowed on the water? That's what they do.[2]
ALBERT: It's just until they leave.
GARY: None of us should approach them until we send word?
ALL: Okay. Yes. Fine.
GARY: Jiliwa that way.
Keep your coolamons full.
It's hot and we need you hydrated.
All agree?
ALBERT: Sure.
GORDON: The plan is—

GARY *holds up his hand.*

GARY: *After* the Welcome, Gordon … Protocols.
GORDON: Sure.

I wish to welcome you to country, the land which provides for us, our Elders, who guide us with their wisdom of the ages, our warriors, who defend us, the stories and ceremonies, which teach us lore. And I welcome you, the respected Elders of the surrounding nations.

JOSEPH: Joseph, Headlands of the Bay Nation. Spear Clan.

ALBERT: Albert, South Shore Nation.

WALTER: Walter, Eel mob, River Nation.

JACOB: Jacob, North Shore Nation. We're lovers and fighters. We love fighting—ay.[3]

GARY: Gary, Northern River Nation.

GORDON: Gordon, proud Harbour and Freshwater Nation.

GARY: Thank you, Gordon, for permission to hold this meeting on your country. Are we happy to speak this common language?[4]

JACOB: Of course!

ALL: Yes. Yep.

GARY: Wait. Where's the Bay mob? Uncle Raymond?

JOSEPH: He declined.

GARY: Why's that, Gordon?

GORDON: Why ask me?

JACOB: You flogged him, hey, bros. What for?

GORDON: Running off his mouth.

GARY *looks disapprovingly at both* GORDON *and* JACOB.

GARY: No gossip. All—other than the Bay mob—are here?

ALL: Yes.

GARY: Good. [*In language*] May the spirits look kindly on this Council of Elders and guide us in our business today.

Gordon, as this is in your country that we meet on—

JACOB: Then why isn't he chairing the meeting?

GARY: Because it's my turn. We agreed last meeting—?

GORDON: But my country has the best lookouts.

They all turn to look out to sea. After a time ...

JOSEPH: Let me get it straight. There were three, but smaller nowees. They left. Now there's one big one?

A few of the men nod in reply.

ALBERT: I've estimated it could hold a whole clan group.

GARY: Hold that great observation, Albert. Our agenda …
JACOB: Keep the river flowing, Gary.
GARY: Actually there's only one item—

There's a sound through the trees and they all react, alert.

LAWRENCE *bursts into the space, panting.*

LAWRENCE: Uncles, Uncles.
GORDON: Warra warra wai.
GARY: Go away.
JACOB: This is men's business.
GARY: Why are you here?
LAWRENCE: Uncle Raymond sent me.
ALBERT: He's Bay mob. Young Lawrence.
GARY: Go on then.

LAWRENCE *is still out of breath …*

LAWRENCE: He wanted me to tell youse about the big nowees …

▼ ▼ ▼

JACOB: One big nowee. We see it.
LAWRENCE: Nah, there's a whole mob of them. Uncle wanted me to warn you.
WALTER: Warn us?
LAWRENCE: That they're coming. That they're on their way. Each with a big mob on board.
GARY: So why isn't *he* here to warn us?

LAWRENCE *quickly glances at* GORDON *and shakes his head.*

LAWRENCE: Umm …
GORDON: He sent a boy in his place.
GARY: I'm not sure about this.
JACOB: At least he's strong.
GORDON: And he's armed.
JOSEPH: Good for him to sit and listen, eh?
JACOB: We can use him to run messages. Hang back there, young fella.
GARY: For the boy's sake, let's go around and introduce ourselves—
GORDON: We've done that. He can catch up.
GARY: Okay … Lawrence, I'm Gary, Chair of this Elders committee.

Who are you, in relation to us? Do you have obligations?

He looks between LAWRENCE *and* ALBERT. *They nod.*

ALBERT: He's my second wife's second cousin's kid. [*As if that explains it all.*]

LAWRENCE: Cousin brother.

ALBERT: Bay mob. Fire Clan.

JOSEPH: Welcome.

GORDON: Oi! That's for me to do. Welcome.

LAWRENCE: Respect to your country, Uncle.

LAWRENCE *nods then sneezes.*

JOSEPH: The dust?

LAWRENCE: The heat. I reckon it's the heat.

LAWRENCE *wipes his mucousy nose on his arm; the others wrinkle their noses in disgust.*

JOSEPH: A scarlet parakeet fell from the sky. In my many years, I have not witnessed that. I wondered … well … could it have something to do with *them*?

JACOB: They don't have that much power, Gramps.

JOSEPH: Perhaps not.

GORDON *clears his throat and* GARY *gets the hint.*

GARY: Gentlemen! This is not our usual, seasonal meeting—

JOSEPH: Being law time. And the women being off on their business—

GARY: —I felt it was incumbent upon me, as Chair, that we should meet to discuss—and agree on—a course of action. Gordon, respectfully, as this is your country, I pass the message stick to you.

GORDON: The plan—

LAWRENCE: Sorry, Uncle Gary?

GARY: Yes, Lawrence?

LAWRENCE: Am I, ah, allowed to ask something?

JACOB: For fuck's sake!

GARY: Jacob!

GORDON: Gadi burns, while we educate a boy.

JOSEPH: Isn't that what we do?

GARY: Gadi's not burning. Nothing's happened.

JACOB: Yet.

GARY: Go ahead.

LAWRENCE: I just want to clarify, why are you meeting? What do you have to agree on?

GARY: Oh, I'm sorry. How we're gunna deal with this mari nowee, this time.

ALBERT: Back after eighteen hot seasons.

JOSEPH: Hot alright.

GORDON: We're gunna scare it away.

ALBERT: Shoo it off, proper way.

LAWRENCE: Oh. Okay then.

JOSEPH: [*to* LAWRENCE] Did Uncle give you any instructions?

LAWRENCE: Oh … yes … Uncle said, if I had a chance, that I should vote, to represent our mob …

GARY: Not sure about that. JACOB: Bit cheeky.

ALBERT: We'll see.

GORDON: Who cares if he votes? What I wanna know is, will he man up? We need the young fellas to form our front line. You up for that?

LAWRENCE: Sure. I brought my spear, my woomera and Uncle's shield.

But he's wary.

JACOB: Ay, look out. Young fella's armed and dangerous!

JOSEPH: Or maybe he can be lookout. Young eyes.

GARY: Please. Let's go about this in an orderly way.

JACOB: Yeah, yeah—

GARY: Our business today is to discuss the nowee—

JACOB: The *mari* nowee.

GARY: Yes, Jacob. The very big nowee. We have eyes, Jacob.

GORDON: The mari nowee that should just warra warra wai out of my country.[5]

GARY: Our process needs to be—

JACOB: Quick. I've got bark for a canoe drying out.[6] In this weather, it'll crack. So, Mr Chair, get on with it!

LAWRENCE: Does anyone know why they're back? After fourteen hot seasons?

WALTER: Fine question, lad.

GARY: It's actually eighteen seasons.

JOSEPH: Well. They come and they go.

JACOB: Who cares why? They're here now. And we want them gone.
GORDON: None of us want them here. Trampling over country. Again.
GARY: Let's put it to a vote. Anyone abstaining?
ALL: No.
GARY: The vote is: we're gunna to send them on their way. Shoo them off. Agreed?
ALL EXCEPT WALTER: Yep.

But they don't notice.

GARY: With a show of force? Yep?

All nod. It seems.

JACOB: Too right.
GARY: Agreed. Make it look like we're serious.
GORDON: We are serious.
ALBERT: Exactly. Mr Chair. I believe Gordon has formulated a plan?
GARY: Gordon, could you set the scene please …

GARY *passes the message stick down to* GORDON, *who accepts it very formally.*

GORDON: Certainly, Mr Chair. I'm suggesting: the attack should come from three directions. Albert, you and South Shore mob, you come from the west side.
ALBERT: My men are on standby. Awaiting my signal.
GORDON: Good fella. Jacob's mob will come down from the east.
JACOB: I have seventy, eighty fellas on standby. Raring to go.
GORDON: And I will bring my fellas over from the south. [*To* JOSEPH] And you, Grandfather. You have your youngest, strongest warriors at the ready?

JACOB *sniggers.*

JOSEPH: Well I, I um …
JACOB: Not much fire power in his mob. Which is—what's the word?—anyway, weird? Coz he's Spear Clan. Haha.
JOSEPH: Ironic?
JACOB: That's not a word.
GARY: What's with you mob, today? You're all over the place!

He shakes his head.

GORDON: And, Walter, your fellas can be in the second wave to come up over the top. That way it looks like there are waves and waves of warriors, never ending.

▼ ▼ ▼

JACOB: Classic strategy.
GARY: Sounds like a plan.
WALTER: Wait.
GARY: What?
ALBERT: Got a different plan?
WALTER: A show of hands?
GARY: What?
WALTER: Before. When you declared that we'd all agreed to shoo them off. The protocol is we vote with a show of hands.
GARY: Okay. Point taken.

They start to put hands up gammon way.

JACOB: [*aside*] He's more of a stickler for the rules than Gazza. [*Under his breath*] And that's saying something.
GARY: [*clearing his throat*] Elders. With a show of hands—all those in favour of sending them away—
GORDON: Once and for all!

Five hands go up. WALTER *does not raise his hand. They all look at him.*

ALBERT: What?
GARY: Why?
JACOB: That's crazy.
GORDON: It's bullshit.
ALBERT: Is this part of some other idea? You got a better idea? He's pretty clever.
WALTER: No.
GARY: [to WALTER] Let me get this straight. You don't want to shoo them away? What do you expect us to do? Set fire to their nowee?
JACOB: Not a bad idea, Gary.
WALTER: No.
GARY: Then what?
ALBERT: Let them land?

WALTER *looks out at the boats. The clouds get darker. A wind whips up.*

WALTER: Maybe.

JACOB: Whaaat?

GORDON: Somebody thinks different.

LAWRENCE: Yeah!

JACOB: It's hot, it's gunna thunder. It's gunna bucket down. We all know what we gotta do.

JOSEPH: There is no precipitation with mammatus clouds. That comes later. With cumulonimbus clouds.

JACOB: Excuse *me*.

GARY: Gentlemen! Keep it nice.

ALBERT *turns to* WALTER.

ALBERT: Is it like he said, are you just trying to be different?

WALTER: No.

ALBERT: Then why?

GORDON: Come on. I mean, they're a pathetic mob.

WALTER: Pathetic. Yes.

GARY: Why don't you want to send them on their way?

▼ ▼ ▼

JOSEPH: What are you seeing, Walter, that we might have missed?

WALTER: They look desperate.[7]

JACOB: How's that our problem?

WALTER: They're in our waters. So they're our responsibility.

GORDON: Not mine.

ALBERT: Look, Walter, from all the stories our old people tell us, we don't want that mob landing. You must have heard those stories? I can tell you—

WALTER: No need.

GARY: So why'd you vote the other way?

WALTER: Well, it might seem simple to just send them away. But it could be a matter of life or death.

JACOB: Don't be ridiculous! We're not gunna die.

GARY: It's a show of force, not an actual battle. A gammon battle.

GORDON: Although we may need to follow through—

ALBERT: If it comes to that.

GORDON: In which case, there's always casualties with war.

GARY: War? That's a whole different set of protocols—we need to check that with the women—no way could we make a decision like that without the women.

WALTER: I wasn't talking about *us* dying. I mean *them*.

He points his lips in the direction of the sea.

And it's daunting to condemn them to death without a discussion first.

ALBERT: How?

WALTER: They could die of hunger or—

JACOB: —or plain *stupidity*. But why should that matter to us?[8]

▼ ▼ ▼

ALBERT: I'm curious as to your evidence for that viewpoint. What's convinced you that they're at risk?

WALTER: Albert—you say evidence? What evidence do *you* have that they aren't? That's my point. Logic suggests we need to check them out first ... then decide.

They all gaze in their direction, but not JACOB *or* GORDON.

The weather changes slightly, as do the clouds and sounds.

GARY: Look. Just because I want to send them off, that doesn't mean I want them to die. I just want them to go away.

JACOB: They don't belong here.

GARY: My mind is made up. All of our minds are fixed, right?

ALL EXCEPT JOSEPH: Right.

JACOB: Even yours, Grandfather, right? Right? Right, Joey?

JOSEPH: Right ... yeah, yeah.

JACOB: And talking about it for a whole mob of seasons won't change our minds.

WALTER: If we talk it through then I would feel we had made an informed decision.

JOSEPH: That's reasonable.

WALTER: It's about us. Following through with our protocols. Which might include us letting them land.

GARY: Serious? You know what that means. We let them land ...

JOSEPH: And we're obliged to welcome them.
JACOB: Haha. Walter. Good one.

WALTER *shrugs.*

GORDON: Welcome them? I've never heard such bullshit.
JACOB: Perhaps he thinks we should invite them to share wallaby? Perhaps we should have a big corroboree for them. Give them access to our best waterholes. Tell 'em to help themselves to our oysters and sand cockles and Goolwa cockles—
GARY: A barbecue.
GORDON: That'd be right! What a joker.
JACOB: I thought I was the joker.
GARY: Shut up, Jacob.
LAWRENCE: You Elders!
ALBERT: Shh.
GARY: Settle down! Hand the message stick to Walter. Explain yourself.

The message stick is passed down.

Go on, Walter. You've got the stick—make it count.
WALTER: Who are we, around this circle? Yes, we're the warriors of our mobs. We're the craftsmen. Scientists, Healers. We're cultured. We have language, more than one. We trade. We have ceremonies and songs. We have lore. We have protocols. And we share one particular protocol, and that is we welcome those who pass through our country.
JOSEPH: True.
WALTER: Our tradition—our protocol—is to welcome visitors to country. We at least owe them that.
GORDON: Don't think so, brother. We have no obligations toward them. And they've got their big nowees to sail in—
JACOB: So they can nowee somewhere else.
GORDON: I don't want them landing on my country. Look, I know their kind. You can't trust 'em. Everybody knows that.
JOSEPH: Pardon me, sir, but how can you slander a whole mob like that?
GORDON: Saying it like it is.
JOSEPH: That doesn't represent my position, my feelings, at all.
GORDON: Are you lecturing me, old fella?
GARY: Ayyyye!
ALBERT: That's not on, Gordon.

JOSEPH: [*to* ALBERT] I'm the senior Elder here.

GARY: Gordon—

GORDON: Sorry, Grandfather.

ALBERT: It's unusual circumstances.

LAWRENCE: On account of the heat and all?

JOSEPH: [*to* LAWRENCE] Please don't think that's how we usually act.

LAWRENCE: Sure, Grandfather.

GARY: In an oyster shell, what are you suggesting, Walter?

WALTER: Rather than just rushing in to confront them, we consider other options. That's what these meetings are for. To consider. We set aside a day, to talk, to listen, to observe.

JACOB: A day? A whole freaking day!

GARY: Calm down! He's right. Our role here is to look at the situation wisely.

ALBERT: That means sticking to what we can prove, what we know.

GARY: Exactly. Orderly, calmly, listening deeply.

ALBERT: Still keeping an eye on them …

LAWRENCE *points but they ignore him.*

JOSEPH: And if it's only a day, and if there's a risk they might die …

LAWRENCE *points more energetically. They ignore him.*

LAWRENCE: Hey, Uncs. Look …

ALBERT: Three of them.

GARY: Three …

GORDON: That's more than last time.

LAWRENCE: There were almost two mobs of them in my country last week …

JOSEPH: Almost two mobs? Twelve?

LAWRENCE: Almost.

GORDON: We need to assemble. We need to prepare.

GARY: We still outnumber them, don't we? All our mobs, against three nowees' of them …?

GORDON: We should be ready to pounce!

JACOB: This meeting should be about the plan, Gary.

ALBERT: We need to be signalling to our men on standby. We need to be briefing them.

GORDON: Prepping them for the battle ahead.

JACOB: Then we can all go home.
LAWRENCE: *Battle*. Yeah! Then I'll be a big man.
JOSEPH: Is that your last test, young fella?
LAWRENCE: Yep. I've gone through most of initiation. Last thing I need to do.[9]

> GORDON *looks at* LAWRENCE *as if for the first time. The others all look pointedly at* GARY.

GARY: Hey! Persuade *him* right way. The vote needs to be unanimous.
GORDON: Gary, can I have a word?

> *Reluctantly,* GARY *goes off with* GORDON *for a moment.*

> GORDON *talks animatedly for a few minutes, while* GARY *looks uncomfortable. The others talk small talk: 'How's the family?' 'How ya bin?' et cetera.*

> JACOB *draws* JOSEPH *off to the side.*

JACOB: Gramps. Got a minute? It's about the new wife.
JOSEPH: Yes.
JACOB: Well. You know.
JOSEPH: No.
JACOB: Well. Things aren't all that … things aren't exactly …
JOSEPH: Oh, oh, I get ya. Well then, let me look at you. Put your arms out.

> JACOB *obliges.* JOSEPH *sniffs under his armpits.*

JACOB: I don't have this trouble with the others … This new one, she's a bit tricky … Ever had that problem?
JOSEPH: Yeah. Nah. Poke ya tongue out.

> *He examines the tongue.*

Hmm. Hmm.
JACOB: What is it? Is it serious?
JOSEPH: Depends. I reckon …
JACOB: Tell me.
JOSEPH: I reckon … she just doesn't like you.

> *He notices everyone's back to the table.*

Oh—they're back.

JOSEPH *re-joins the others, a crestfallen* JACOB *slinking along behind.* GORDON *stands, addressing the others.*

GORDON: I'm proposing that the young fella can vote. We all have times when there is sorry business, or other business, when we send an Elder-in-training to represent our mob, eh?

ALBERT: Hmm …

GARY: Gordon has convinced me that there are precedents.

ALBERT: It's unusual—

JACOB: Like everything about this crazy day—

JOSEPH: The wind's picking up. Hear it?

▼ ▼ ▼

GARY: Albert?

ALBERT: I suppose.

GARY: Grandfather?

JOSEPH: I guess … why not?

WALTER: I'm okay with it. We agree then?

ALL: Yes.

WALTER: With a show of hands?

GARY: With a show of hands.

All hands go up.

GORDON: Welcome, son.

LAWRENCE: Thanks. Unc.

But he's wary.

WALTER: Mr Chair, can we observe them for a few moments? Indulge me.

JACOB: Why don't we watch them for the next five seasons so you can get everything straight?

ALBERT: Why are you so interested in them?

JACOB: Yeah, what's that about?

WALTER: I'm interested in what we can learn from them.

JACOB: Not much.

WALTER: Us mob exchange knowledge all the time.[10]

ALBERT: That's how we make sense of the world, isn't it? As scientists? By exchanging knowledge.

WALTER: Then why not with them?

But ALBERT *shakes his head.*

GARY: Okay, okay. Let's all observe them for a few minutes.
JACOB: Why don't we measure their heads while we're at it?

They all just stare out. After some time ...

[*To* GORDON] Tap me on the shoulder when something happens.
GORDON: Nothing's gunna happen.
GARY: So why the scare campaign then, Gordon?

After a time ...

ALBERT: What have we learnt?
JACOB: Lot of bark in those nowees.
GARY: That they appear to be watching us?
JOSEPH: Maybe they're waiting for us to welcome them? Do you see any Elders on board ...?
GORDON: They don't have Elders.
JOSEPH: Ttt.
ALBERT: Anything solid? Like solid *evidence*? That we can use to form an opinion?
LAWRENCE: [*boldly*] You've checked them out, Uncle. What have you learned?
WALTER: There's at least two clan groups. The ones with the ceremonial markings. And the other group.[11]
ALBERT: Yes. But what does that mean?
GORDON: Different to last time.
GARY: Anything else?

They look at each other, look across the sea, look back at each other. The sounds of masts creaking, and metal on metal, and faint voices.

JOSEPH: They're noisy buggers.

Sniggers of laughter.

GARY: Okay, okay ... let's try a different tack. Let's all take a small mob of time to yarn Walter around.
JACOB: Like a really small mob of time. No bloody speeches, right?
GARY: Stop interrupting. We each take a small mob of time to put forward our arguments. Why we should scare them off. Who'll begin? Grandfather Joseph, as the eldest?

JOSEPH: Please, not yet.

GARY: Lawrence?

JACOB: You set a grass fire, young fella, we'll see what it flushes out.

GORDON: But watch which way the wind is blowing.

LAWRENCE: Uncle Raymond said … well, I think …

GARY: Go on.

LAWRENCE: Well, their nowees were in my country for three days.

GARY: Yeah, almost twelve of them [*snorting in derision*]. Go on.

LAWRENCE: They came onto country and cut a heap of grass and took it back to their nowees. They needed help to find water.[12] They're a bit … I dunno, not very savvy, I guess. Uncle Raymond says we should send them away. He says they don't belong. They are myall, strangers.

WALTER: Yet we welcome everyone else. That's our way of doing things since, well, the beginning of time.

LAWRENCE: Well, sure … I know what it is to welcome a visitor to my country. I mean … I'm not an Elder, not yet but …

WALTER: A welcome is a welcome.

LAWRENCE: What I'm trying to say is, I don't think it's the same with them. They're different.

JACOB: Sure are.

WALTER: Different doesn't mean less than.

GARY: We don't know that. Let's not speculate.

ALBERT: Better to draw upon our *knowledge* of them. What do we know—first-hand?

They all look at each other. They all look blank.

WALTER: I have something.

JACOB: Is it 'magic'? Haha.

WALTER: Kind of.

WALTER *brings out a tomahawk. They come over to look,* GORDON *holding back.*

ALBERT: Is that a mago?[13]

WALTER: Kind of.

LAWRENCE *touches it.*

LAWRENCE: It's sharp!

GARY: Don't cut yourself, young fella!
ALBERT: Where'd you get it?
WALTER: I found it. After they left last time …
JACOB: Weird.

They begin to fool around with it.

JOSEPH: It's not flint. Or greenstone. What would you use it for, Jacob?
JACOB: I'd use it for fighting.
WALTER: I experimented with it. Say you have a possum that has fled up onto a branch—
JACOB: The women do that. That's their job—
WALTER: With this implement you can chop down that branch really quickly, and get to the possum, in just a few blows.
ALBERT: *Incredible!*
LAWRENCE: Awesome.
JACOB: Yeah, yeah. I like it.
JOSEPH: But if you chop down the branch, isn't it gone forever?
WALTER: That's true, so like all tools, one must be judicious in its use.

▼ ▼ ▼

JACOB: I could trade with you. I have some excellent spears.[14]

WALTER *ignores him.*

LAWRENCE: Hey, Unc. Don't give it to these old fellas, no disrespect. It's a young fella thing. New *technology*.
WALTER: Exactly! Or say you're running up a tree, to get honey—
JACOB: The women collect the honey.
WALTER: —and it is painstaking to make the notches in the side of the tree, this is perfect for making the notches—like this.[15]

He demonstrates making a notch in the timber.

See?
JOSEPH: In terms of it using less time, what do we do with the extra time we save?
WALTER: That's a point too.
JACOB: There must be something I can trade. A wife …
WALTER: No thanks. Albert? What do you make of it?
ALBERT: It's very much like our magos, the stuff it's made from except maybe—and I hate to say this, but better?

GORDON: Big deal.
WALTER: Jacob?
JACOB: I'd use it.
LAWRENCE: I really want it.
GORDON: Pff. You lot are gullible. Sucked in by a toy.
ALBERT: They might have other—what did you call it? Technologies. We don't know.
WALTER: Gary, don't you have something of theirs?

▼ ▼ ▼

GARY: Thanks, Walter … They gave my wife's Aunty this.[16]

He pulls a faded red ribbon from his pocket.

[*Apologetically*] I sometimes use it to tie the feet of fowl together. It's quite strong.
WALTER: And wasn't there something about a cloth?
GARY: Now that you remind me, yes … they also gave her this.

He pulls out a handkerchief and covers his groin area with it.[17] JACOB *begins to laugh. They all join in.* GARY *hams it up a little, enjoying the attention, doing a coy dance.*

JOSEPH: Your wife's Aunty didn't feel threatened?
ALBERT: They didn't try to drag away any of the women?
GARY: Why, no.
ALBERT: Of course that doesn't mean that they wouldn't. Just that they didn't. On that occasion.
WALTER: That's right. They didn't.
JACOB: How is he so sure?
GORDON: When he hasn't even been up close.
GARY: Well, what do you know *for sure* then, Gordon?
GORDON: Last time they were aggressive. I know that *first-hand*. They had many weapons. Goorabeeras.[18]
LAWRENCE: Like you, Uncle?
JACOB: Cheeky!
GARY: You were there? Tell us. Pass him the message stick.

The message stick is passed to GORDON. *But he won't take it.*

GORDON: Was a long time ago.
ALBERT: The illalong with the hole! I know this story! Gary, pass it!

LAWRENCE *passes* ALBERT *the shield.*

JACOB: We all know it.

He sighs.

ALBERT: And the message stick, Lawrence … So, eighteen summers ago—

JACOB: [*groaning*] No speeches …

ALBERT: Eighteen hot seasons ago, this same mob. with the same markings, appear. The Elders try to ignore them, but they kept persisting. So they sent down an advance party. Uncle George, Gordon's father, and Uncle Raymond.

LAWRENCE: Uncle Raymond tells this yarn!

ALBERT: Except he was young Raymond then.

GORDON: Raymond shouldn't be telling that story.

GARY: Then you tell it.

But GORDON *shakes his head and* ALBERT *grabs his chance to continue.*

ALBERT: It's a community story and I have the message stick. The two men step forward but in response the goorabeera erupts, Bang! frightening the cockatoos from the trees. Old Uncle George get a big fright.[19] A poisonous smell lingers in the air … Second time, the goorabeera rings out again. Bang! Old Uncle George is struck in the leg! He bleeds! He gives out a terrifying yell. Brave Uncle Raymond—[20]

GORDON *reacts* ...

GORDON: You're telling that story wrong.

... *but* ALBERT *is intent* ...

ALBERT: Brave young Raymond with his spear and his illalong charges towards them. The goorabeera bangs once more and this was the result!

He holds LAWRENCE*'s shield up and puts his finger through a hole.*[21] *They all nod—except* GORDON *and* WALTER.

Straight through it went!

▼▼▼

LAWRENCE: I like the way you tell that story.

GORDON *growls.*

WALTER: Mmmmm. That story's …

ALBERT: The point is: those things hurt from a whole mob of distance. And we have proof. Bang!

JOSEPH: Old Uncle repelled them though?

GARY: Obviously. They left. But now they're back. Do we want that to happen again?

ALBERT: No.

JOSEPH: No.

JACOB: We need more than two old fellas to scare them off.

He goes to stand up but WALTER *holds up his hand.*

WALTER: Wait! What if there's another explanation?

GARY: [*to* WALTER] You have questions, well so do I. Like, why the need for the goorabeera? When old Uncle was approaching them to talk?

GORDON: To *welcome* them.

GARY: Explain that!

WALTER: I can't.

ALBERT: You say that a lot, Walter.

WALTER: Yes.

ALBERT *points to the shield reverentially.*

▼▼▼

ALBERT: This is the very illalong that was pierced by the goorabeera. We have the story, but we can also see the outcome with our own eyes.

WALTER: That story. There's something wrong …

GORDON: [*muttering*] Yes.

GARY: Go on.

WALTER: What if that hole, in that illalong, wasn't caused by a goorabeera?

ALBERT: Look at it! It wasn't made by a piece of flint or a kangaroo tooth. It wasn't made by anything we know. Yet there's a hole.

GORDON: The goorabeera made that hole. I swear on my life.

WALTER: Perhaps there's a different explanation?

WALTER *reveals his shield. There is a hole in it. Everyone stares at it.*

GORDON: It's a trick.

JOSEPH: My eyes tell me that's the same kind of hole!

JACOB: Did you find that too? After they left?

WALTER: No. It's mine. And I made the hole in it.

ALBERT: How?

WALTER: Using an object of theirs that I found.

JACOB: You love their stuff.

WALTER: At first I wasn't sure what it was, and if it was utilitarian or a trivial thing. I experimented and discovered it was a tool. It's perfect for making these kinds of openings—it's very hard—and it can make unusual markings. See?

He shows the decoration on his shield.

JACOB: That tool, you still got it?

GORDON: Lies. All lies.

WALTER: You said the hole in the illalong proved they were dangerous.

GORDON: That mob is dangerous. I know it.

WALTER: What if the story's exaggerated?

LAWRENCE: What do you mean?

WALTER *turns to* ALBERT.

WALTER: Albert, is what I said possible?

ALBERT: Those old stories are evidence.

WALTER: Then perhaps my story is too? [*To* JOSEPH] What about you, Grandfather? Do you still think Albert's tale is the whole, and the only, story?

JOSEPH: It's a mystery.

GARY: Or a distraction. We need to decide whether we let them land or not. Gordon says they're dangerous: Walter says they're not. What else do we have?

WALTER: I said, 'They're not *necessarily* dangerous'.

GARY: Could they … if we let them land, would it be possible that they could deny us our liberty?[22]

GORDON: Pff. They won't succeed. I am the equal of three of those people. In my opinion, they are weak, dull and cowardly.

JACOB: If they try to rush us, we'll respond in force. They won't know what hit them.

GORDON: In terms of marksmanship, they have no idea of our superiority over them.[23] We have more accurate spears, and more athletic warriors.[24]

WALTER: That also contradicts your story about the goorabeera, and their terrifying 'magical' powers. Therefore they prove no threat.

GORDON: You're trying to trip me up.

JOSEPH: Gentlemen!

GORDON: None of us want them here.

Sullen silence.

▼ ▼ ▼

GORDON: Bay mob fella said they tossed their dead overboard, at dawn.[25]

GARY: I heard it was one body.

GORDON: So? Still not right.

WALTER: Gordon. You fight with that family group, don't you?

LAWRENCE: Hey. That's my mob—

GARY: Shush, young fella!

WALTER: You speak of their dishonesty often, yet, all of a sudden, this Bay mob brother is a reliable witness.

GORDON *stands up.*

GORDON: You think you're a real clever fella.

WALTER: I am the clever fella.

GARY: Gordon! Elders!

He has a migraine.

Grandfather, Joseph, I would really value your wise council right now ...

JOSEPH: Still gathering my thoughts.

GARY: That's okay, Grandfather. Take your time.

JACOB: Like we've got lots of that.

WALTER: We have as long as it takes. We have forever.

JACOB: [*under his breath*] We're gunna use up our forever yabbering.

GARY: Alright then—Jacob, your turn.

ALBERT *tosses him the message stick.*

JACOB: Why yarn up big time about them? You've checked them out. They are among the miserablest specimens you've ever seen. Wretched.[26]

JOSEPH: Have you seen their teeth?

▼ ▼ ▼

LAWRENCE: Their teeth are shocking.[27]

ALBERT: You have to be up quite close to notice their teeth.

GORDON: Teeth? *Teeth?!* I mean, come on, we need to take action! Before they … before they … ambush us. Jacob—c'mon. Do something, bros.

JACOB: [*to* WALTER] We all want to send them away. You're stopping us. Why?

WALTER: Alright. I have a peculiar feeling about this. And too many questions that I don't have the answers for. For instance, we don't know what their motivations are. They could have come in peace, they could be in trouble, they could offer us things that are useful.

JACOB: Peculiar feeling? It's about a feeling? And their motivations? Seriously?

He laughs and GORDON *joins in.*

GORDON: Nothing you say changes what I see with my own eyes.
I see big nowees. Lots of them.
I see a mob of mobs of people.
Dangerous people.

LAWRENCE: There's another one!

ALBERT: Four nowees.

LAWRENCE: And another on the horizon!

GARY: That'll make five.

JOSEPH: Maybe he was right? About the two mobs.

He points at LAWRENCE. *They all look out at sea.*

ALBERT: They're so big. Huge.

LAWRENCE: Taller than ten men.

GARY: Elders? Elders! Your arguments?

GORDON: The goorabeeras. That's all the evidence we need.

WALTER: We haven't actually seen any goorabeeras, this time.

▼▼▼

ALBERT: Technically, we haven't seen anything and they haven't done anything.

GORDON: Why are you siding with him?

ALBERT: I'm not.

There is thunder in the distance. The wind has picked up.

JOSEPH: Cumulonimbus clouds. Wild weather is imminent, gentlemen.[28]

GARY: Grandfather, it must be your turn. Please. Have you formulated your thoughts?

JOSEPH: Shouldn't we go back to our women? Hear what they have to say?

ALBERT: Our women are on secret business. They were firm about us not bothering them.

JOSEPH: Right.

JACOB *groans. There is long silence, and then suddenly everyone begins talking at once—overlapping.*

GORDON: Did anyone force them to come here? No—!

JACOB: If they die, whose fault is that? Not ours—

ALBERT: And what about the trees? They hacked them down, last time. They just swept through ceremonial grounds—

JACOB: All this talk talk talk. Yabba yabba.

GARY: Quiet.

JOSEPH: I can't hear myself think—

ALBERT: They slashed trees on one side—

JACOB: When some of us would rather be elsewhere!

GARY: Quiet!

ALBERT: —muddied the streams—

JACOB: Me in particular—as well as the canoe, I've got that new wife—

GARY: Busy man—

JACOB: Too right—

JOSEPH: I can't hear myself *think*!

GARY: Elders! Quiet. Men. Brothers! Shut up!

They all fall silent.

LAWRENCE: Do youse have to yell? You're giving me a headache.

They look at him, but basically they're too caught up in their own mire.

And how do you agree on anything?

ALBERT: [*to* WALTER, *quieter*] You've managed to stir up all this chaos over something that should be really straightforward.

GORDON: None of us want them here.

JOSEPH: You don't speak for everyone. Not for me, anyway.

GORDON: Old man!

GARY: Gordon.

JACOB: Fellas, let's just decide.

GARY: It can't just be any old decision. Has to be the right one. And sometimes these things take time. Middens weren't built in a day. Walter, have you got anything to add?

Pause.

GORDON: He's got nothing. Let's go. Let's do it.

They all stand as if to leave, excepting GARY *and* JOSEPH.

GARY: Wait!

GORDON: I'm going down there now. C'mon, men.

GARY: We haven't voted …

GORDON, JACOB *and* ALBERT *are gathering their things when* WALTER *speaks softly.*

WALTER: Stop. I'll do you a deal. You vote. I'll sit it out. If you all vote to repel them, I'll respect the decision.

GARY: Highly unusual. But then, this is a most unusual meeting … Any objections?

ALL: No … let's do it … about time …

JACOB: Deadly! Let's get it over with.

ALBERT: It'll move things along.

GORDON: Some action.

WALTER *walks over to the lookout point, intensely still, and then turns, observing them.*

GARY: Last time, Brother Walter was ostracised by the way he voted. I don't use that word lightly. So this time we will vote anonymously. Each of you, mark the message stick. To send them away, mark the red section. To let them land, mark the yellow section. Clear?

He marks the stick with a piece of sharp flint then passes both on. The movement of the clouds across the sky quickens as if time has sped up. One by one, they make their mark on the stick. Finally it reaches GARY *again.*

Walter?

WALTER *returns.* GARY *examines the stick carefully.*

Send them away.
Away.
Away.
Away.
Away.
One mark indicating we should allow them to land …

GORDON *bangs his boomerangs together.*

GORDON: That's a joke!
JACOB: Which one of you? Own up. The rest of us deserve to know.
GARY: The point of a secret ballot is that we don't disclose the way we vote. If the Elder wants it that way …
GORDON: He doesn't need to own up. We all know who turned.

He points at JOSEPH.

Hey, Grandfather? One heartbeat you are voting to send them back to where they came from and the next this smooth-talking do-gooder is spinning a story about a poor mob who are gunna die if we don't help them, so you jump over to the other side of the river. That's pathetic.
GARY: Hey! We don't talk to each other like that! We're Elders. It's not right.
GORDON: You're worried about what's right? We're trying to send this ruthless mob back to where they belong—and all of a sudden we're paying attention to a pack of stories!
JOSEPH: Please—
GARY: Gordon!
JOSEPH: Please—
GARY: Can I remind everyone, that this is not about what the 'popular' decision is. I am proud to be an Elder on this Council because I value that we have different opinions and that we talk things through in a respectful manner. Gordon. Your tone is not in the spirit of these meetings.
GORDON: Gunna get the whole set of protocols chanted at us, are we?
GARY: No. Just you.

GORDON, *at boiling point, steps towards* GARY *but* JACOB *intervenes.*

JACOB: Let's get back to this brother. Who changes his mind, just like that.

They all circle JOSEPH.

Tell us why?

ALBERT: Yes, enlighten us.

GORDON: Yeah! Yeah.

JOSEPH: I can't—

GORDON: Coward!

LAWRENCE: Because it was me.

GORDON: You!

JOSEPH: You.

JACOB: Give us your reason!

LAWRENCE: I, I—

GORDON: We're not interested.

GARY: Really? I am. Go on.

GORDON: He's a kid. What does he know? His vote don't count.

WALTER: Gordon—you made us vote to count his vote.

The two men stand chin to chin, one calm, the other livid.

JACOB: Ha, that's funny. He's got you there, Gordon. Backfired big time.

GARY: The vote is five to two. Young fella, explain your logic.

JACOB: He probably likes his five minutes in the overhead sun. His moment around the big fire. With the big boys.

ALBERT: You are mixing your poetic descriptions.

JACOB: Want a spear in the neck?

GARY: Hey!

JACOB: Okay, okay …

GARY: Speak.

LAWRENCE: Perhaps there's some truth in what he says. It's exciting to be heard.

JACOB: Told ya! [*To* GORDON] Hey! I bet it's that business with Raymond—that's what! You've made an enemy of the Bay mob!

GORDON *pushes* LAWRENCE *a little.*

GORDON: Is that it? It's a revenge on me?

LAWRENCE: It's nothing to do with that! Even though I think you're a bully.

GORDON *goes to biff* LAWRENCE *but* WALTER *shoves* LAWRENCE *sideways and stands in his place.*

GARY: [*to* LAWRENCE] And you lot, quit it. Finish what you have to say, Lawrence. [*Under his breath*] The meeting's a fucking shamble.

LAWRENCE: Okay. The reason I changed is—him. [*Pointing at* WALTER] This Uncle chose to be a lone voice. You don't know what it's like to be young. You're always being told what to do. Do this, do that. Everything's for the greater good of the mob …

He has guts to go against the tide. I hear his line of thinking. Those fellas on the nowees? We don't know what they want. Or what they have to offer. Like that tool. Hey, this is the first time out of my country, being with you mob, and I've already learnt so much. What could I learn from them?

JACOB: Big speech, young fella.

GORDON: Some of us are better at actions.

GARY: You understand, young Lawrence, that our vote, it's a serious thing?

LAWRENCE: I'm not stupid. I reckon we should just talk about it some more.

JACOB: How we gunna talk with them goobarras at our throat? [*Pointing to* WALTER] Tell us that.

ALBERT: Walter, have you considered? What if they have come here to do wrong?

JOSEPH: Last time they 'permanently borrowed' forty spears.

LAWRENCE: What do you mean?

JOSEPH: I can't even explain the concept of 'permanently borrowed'.

ALBERT: He means they took them. And didn't put them back.

LAWRENCE: True?

▼▼▼

JOSEPH: I heard a group of them heading my way, noisily, banging and crashing through the bush. Naturally, I wanted to avoid them. I fled, my oysters and mussels still sizzling on the fire. I huddled behind a kurrajong tree, watching. Not only did they nick my lunch,[29] cheeky ones, but they happened upon my mob's spears, and took the lot![30]

JACOB: Explain that!

WALTER: I don't know. It doesn't sound plausible. They must have left something in return? An exchange for something of equal value?[31]

JOSEPH: They left a few useless items. Nowhere near the value of those spears. Which I am still replacing …

GORDON: They have nothing we need.[32]

JACOB: I like that chopping thing.

GORDON: Okay, *that.* But nothing else.

GARY: What if they capture our nowees?

WALTER: Why would they? Look at theirs!

LAWRENCE: Good point.

JOSEPH: There's another story. An old Aunty from my mob said they treated her with kindness, that they shared some maugro with her.

ALBERT: Had they negotiated to fish in that area? Did they take the appropriate quota?

JOSEPH: I cannot say.

JACOB: I heard they took loads and loads. Enough for a corroboree.[33]

GORDON: They slaughtered stingrays—

JACOB: I heard the bay was like a summer's sunset, red with blood.

GORDON: —stingrays as old as my father's father's father.[34]

ALBERT: Don't those things worry you?

WALTER: Of course they do.

JACOB: Let's go back a bit. The whole idea of them being here is a little ridiculous, isn't it? Why aren't they on their own country?

GORDON: That's right. That's true, eh, brother.

JOSEPH: Unless they don't have a country?

JACOB: Rubbish! Everyone has a country. We are not born of the sea, we're born of the land. We belong to the earth. That's who we are, as human beings.

GORDON: That's right. They must.

ALBERT: They should be home, caring for it. That's their responsibility. To their country.

ALL: Yeah. Yep. That's right,

ALBERT: Except, right now, they're here …

GARY: Perhaps they'll go home. Tomorrow.

JOSEPH: They'll be mere specks of dust on the horizon …

ALBERT: We'll be left with funny stories we tell our grandkids …

LAWRENCE: They left my country. Stayed for three days then they left.

They ignore him—until he sneezes three times.

JOSEPH: You are unwell. Your eyes glow, as does your nose.

LAWRENCE: My head aches.

JOSEPH: Green slides from your nose. Like slime at the edge of a waterhole.

JACOB: Too much information!

LAWRENCE *sneezes again and again.*

Enough. You've had your fun.

JOSEPH: He's mimicking them.

ALBERT: You have to get quite close to mimic them.

He looks hard at LAWRENCE.

You're not saying something. *Nephew.*

LAWRENCE: Okay … the night they arrived in my country, my way lit by the full moon, I took my Uncle's nowee in their vicinity. I got up quite close.

GARY: Why the need to get close?

GORDON: [*looking at* JOSEPH] When some people would hide behind a gum tree.

LAWRENCE: I felt it was my duty.

WALTER: You wanted to see them for yourself.

GARY: Curiosity killed the echidna.

LAWRENCE *shrugs.*

LAWRENCE: I'd heard stories, rumours.

WALTER: You wanted to make up your own mind.

LAWRENCE: Yes.

JOSEPH: And?

LAWRENCE: My nowee slid beside theirs. It was like a cliff face. As tall as a fig tree!

He shivers. He has their attention.

The night was still. I could hear snoring. Big mob of snoring.

He mimics the sound. JACOB *laughs.*

JACOB: Sounds like my new wife.

LAWRENCE: And other weird noises …

He mimics a rooster ... They all laugh.

GARY: Maybe they sound like that when they …

He makes a suggestive movement. The others laugh.

JOSEPH: More.

LAWRENCE *mimics a cow ... a sheep ... then a pig. They all laugh.*

JACOB: Again!

He makes the sound of a horse neighing, and a small dog yapping.[35] *Then he whistles the tune of 'For he's a jolly good fellow.'*[36]

GORDON: Fuck this.

LAWRENCE *shuts up.*

ALBERT: So the nowee …

LAWRENCE: It's like an ants' nest. Goes on and on, layers and layers.

JACOB: Wee-eee … [*An aside*] Do they have women on board?

LAWRENCE: Who can tell? Their voices are odd. Soft. 'Go n'eiri an bother leat.' [*Irish Gaelic, pronounced: 'Gah niahrey un bo-her lat'; meaning: 'May the road rise with you', that is, Travel well.*]

GARY: Did you see them? Up close?

LAWRENCE: One of them. Leaning over the nowee.

WALTER: What was he like?

LAWRENCE: His whole demeanour was hideous. Not swathed in a red cloak. This one looked like he had been at war, his cloaks ripped.

WALTER: And?

LAWRENCE: Setting aside their human shape they differ little from brutes. They have stocky bodies, short limbs, narrow heads, thin lips and wide-open protruding eyes that have a fish-like lightness. They are of a very unpleasing aspect, having not one graceful feature in their faces.[37] They have no facial hair, their faces were as smooth as a young girl, I could hardly tell which sex is which.[38]

JOSEPH *is nodding.*

GARY: Not a flattering picture.

GORDON: No. They're ugly.

JOSEPH: That's disrespectful, Gordon.

ALBERT: Did they have anything … unusual? Other *technologies*?

LAWRENCE: Hmm … The one leaning over … he had a small fire stick that smelt acrid. Though not as bad as him! He smelt like death.

JOSEPH: Malodorous.

LAWRENCE: He kept scratching himself. Scratch, scratch. And the smoking activity …

LAWRENCE *breaks off a twig and demonstrates 'smoking a pipe'.*

JOSEPH: Smoking ceremony. Trying to heal himself.

LAWRENCE: And then he …

He sneezes. And sneezes.

JOSEPH: And?

LAWRENCE: I felt a small spray, like mist from a waterfall.

GARY: Curious, but irrelevant.

LAWRENCE: Hey, I'm just explaining.

He is unsettled, feverish.

GORDON: If that fella was in my mob, and we had to travel a long distance, say to the new season's hunting ground, sounds like he wouldn't make it.

WALTER: You'd leave him behind.

GORDON: Hey! Sometimes, that's just the way it is. You give him medicine, you bring in a man of higher degree—like Grandfather—to extract any foreign matter, but if that fails, the man, woman, or child, is done for. You know that. You have to leave them behind. They know that. The whole mob knows that.[39]

ALBERT: Gentlemen, the point is, one or many of them, are showing signs of some calamity. What else?

LAWRENCE *groans a little.*

JOSEPH: Are you okay?

LAWRENCE: The heat. This crazy heat.

A wind whips up and they shiver.

JOSEPH: But it's cooled down now.

ALBERT: If they're unwell …

WALTER: What if someone like Grandfather could cure them?

JOSEPH: Whoa! I'm not sure my powers are that great.

WALTER: But they might be.

JOSEPH: There are certain herbs, particularly, that help with scratching. I could help with that. Actually, I am certain I could. And our smoking ceremonies are fairly advanced.

LAWRENCE: I'm sure you could too, Grandfather.

JACOB: You cured that small problem I had.

JOSEPH: That was nothing. The appropriate fern root, chewed.

JACOB: It wasn't nothing for me, or the wife.

He laughs.

GARY: Wives.

JOSEPH: How many now, brother?

JACOB: Three …

JOSEPH: Wheee.

JACOB: It's a lot of responsibility. Lotta hard work.

ALBERT: Sounds like it. For them. Fishing. Catching possums. Collecting honey …

GARY: With respect … can we get back to *those* folk?

JACOB: You started it.

JOSEPH: Young Lawrence. Were you … alarmed at any time? Did you tremble in their presence?

LAWRENCE: No.

JOSEPH: Me neither.

GARY: What?

JOSEPH *shakes his head.*

LAWRENCE: But afterwards, Uncle Raymond beat me for having risked his nowee. Of course he found out …

He goes to drink from the coolamon but it is empty.

Water's run out …

JOSEPH: They need water! That's why they're here.

WALTER: To fill up their coolamons. They fill up their coolamons and they leave.

LAWRENCE: That's what they did out our way. Filled up their coolamons, cut grass, chopped down a tree. Then left.[40]

JACOB: Bloody hooligans.

WALTER: You can die of thirst. That's what I'm saying.

GARY: Makes sense.

JOSEPH: We have beautiful clear water. While their water is *poisoned.*

GARY: Poor buggers.

Most, excepting GORDON, *get up to look at them.*

GORDON: This is mad.

WALTER: It's risky, them being away from their land. For them and their families and their country. Why would they do that unless they had to? That they had no choice?

ALBERT: Yeah, but we have a choice.

WALTER: Yes.

GARY: [*to* JOSEPH] How do you know their water is poisoned?

JOSEPH: I don't. But when I drank that other mob's—

LAWRENCE: You interacted with them!

JOSEPH: I was foolish!

JACOB: You debil debil, Grandfather!

JOSEPH *looks shame.*

GORDON: Tell us!

▼▼▼

JOSEPH: Okay. That other mob, those other visitors, those ones with the different cloaks? [*Mimicking perfectly*] *'Bonjour, au sauvage!'* They gave me liquid that looked like water, but when you guzzled it … [*Giggling*] 'Fire! Fire! My mouth's on fire!' You wanted to hurl yourself into the river, your tongue hanging from your mouth like a blue-tongue. You couldn't rid yourself of the bitterness.[41]

ALBERT: But they drink it by choice?

JOSEPH: Eagerly.

JACOB: No accounting for taste.

GORDON *snorts.*

JOSEPH: They also shaped my beard and rearranged my hair.[42]

GARY: That's why you look younger!

JOSEPH: It was harmless fun.

WALTER: Grandfather, you say they are harmless yet you still vote to repel them. That strikes me as … inconsistent. And if they are sick, you can help them.

There's a lack of humanity in that. Maybe you're fine about them landing?

JOSEPH: I could be persuaded.

JACOB: Grandfather!

JOSEPH: But then I see the other side too.

LAWRENCE: Do these things always pan out like this?

GARY: Sometimes. JACOB: Always! ALBERT: Never.

LAWRENCE *looks bewildered.*

LAWRENCE: Elders! Look! There's six of them. Six nowees.

They stare out to sea.

ALBERT: Six!

JOSEPH: Six …? A whole mob of them …

GARY: We still outnumber them. All our mobs around the water. Don't we?

ALBERT: You're the numbers man, Gary.

GARY: I reckon that's right.

They all look out to sea—except GORDON.

JOSEPH: Wait! The birds have gone silent.

ALBERT: It's gunna rain. The ants foretold that.

JOSEPH: They were frenzied.

GARY: We should shelter …

It is very quiet. Suddenly, there is a crack of lightning, and the sound of rain.

WALTER: They're restless.

ALBERT: The storm?

LAWRENCE: No. Look.

JOSEPH: What are they doing?

JOSEPH: A ceremony?

*There are the sounds of drums and a fife playing. They listen … ('The Rogue's March')**

GARY: How many are there?

LAWRENCE: I tried to tell you!

Pause as they stare out towards the sea.

JOSEPH: What going on?

GARY: There's a structure like a tree, with a twisted rope. Is it stringybark?

They watch, alarmed. GORDON *rises to join them.*

JACOB: And a man, struggling.

---

* https://www.youtube.com/watch?v=Uap1EF4w9RY
Played when undesirables, both military and civilian, were drummed out of camp, or on their way to punishment. Its origins are uncertain, but it probably dates to the early 18th century.

LAWRENCE: They're putting the rope around his neck! Oh. Oh …
JOSEPH: What?
ALBERT: They're pulling up the rope and …

There is a very faint but bloodcurdling wail.

JOSEPH: I have never heard such an awful sound! Oh, my spirit!
GARY: The man, he's twitching! Thrashing about!

They stare in horror, mesmerised.

JACOB: Still thrashing …

They watch. For a long time ...

ALBERT: He's dead.
LAWRENCE: Finally.
JOSEPH: Dead?
LAWRENCE: He hangs like a skun animal.
JOSEPH: In your wildest thoughts, can you ever think of such a thing?
GARY: The horror.[43]

Silence.

GORDON: [*to* WALTER] You want that to happen to us? We let them on shore, they might do that to us? Look how that man swings, lifeless. Look! Look! *Look!* It's barbaric.
ALBERT: Explain that, Walter.

WALTER *shakes his head.*

WALTER: I can't.
JOSEPH: Could we teach them … other ways?
GORDON: They should be gone. They're brutes.
ALBERT: Are they cracking under some pressure?
WALTER: Maybe being on those nowees. Maybe they're bad camps. They look like they have terrible lives.
JOSEPH: It's making them go wombah. Poor things.
ALBERT: The one who swung, he probably transgressed. So they punished him.
WALTER: It's true that when people don't follow lore, there's consequences.
JACOB: This mob—let's say those fellas have no country and they have no Elders. We can't help that. We can't help it that those nowees are bad camps. A breeding ground for people who don't follow lore.

GORDON: Let them swing on the end of a rope. So what? As long as they don't do that to my mob.
WALTER: So what? Are you their executioner?
GORDON: I could be!
WALTER: Perhaps you'd like to be the one on the end of that rope, pulling it tighter.
GORDON: Are you gammon me? Hand me that rope and I'd yank it tight!
WALTER: I pity you.
GORDON: I'd stop right there …
WALTER: I can't imagine *wanting* to have them swinging from a rope!
GORDON: Be quiet!
WALTER: You're the brute.
GORDON: Be quiet!
WALTER: You want to see each and every one of them wither away. Perhaps out of some hatred for your fellow man?

▼▼▼

GORDON *grabs his spear and raises it at* WALTER, *but two of the others leap up and put him and his arm away. He fights them as* WALTER *watches calmly.*

GORDON: Let me at him. I'll spear him. I'll spear him!
WALTER: That's what you want? To spear me?

GORDON *is pent-up with anger.* JACOB *tries to sooth him.*

JACOB: He's trying to rile you, cuz. He's poking around the ants' nest.

Uncomfortable pause.

ALBERT: If he was a transgressor, then they dealt with him.
JOSEPH: But he had no chance to learn his lesson.
JACOB: He should've been speared. Nothing like a nice clean spearing.
GORDON: You said it. Transgressors should be speared.
JOSEPH: Hey! I was begat from a transgressor. My father, he married wrong skin. Perhaps I am tainted with his sin?
GARY: It wasn't meant personally.
JOSEPH: It sounds personal.
ALBERT: Grandfather, he was referring to the *situation*, that's all.
JOSEPH: I feel sorry for them. When we have so much. Our lives are so much better.[44]

JACOB: You go and share your kangaroo tail with them. Go ahead.

JOSEPH *stares at him, then puts his hand up.*

JOSEPH: I'm changing my vote—

JACOB: How the wind just turns direction, just like—that!

JOSEPH: The wind does change direction. See, now it's onshore.

JACOB: Yeah, and I smell their stench!

GARY: Let him speak! Grandfather …

JOSEPH: It's like Walter says—everyone should be given a chance. No matter where they come from.

GARY: Are you sure?

JOSEPH: I think so. Yes.

ALBERT: You need to be certain.

JOSEPH: Excuse me—I am. And …

WALTER: Yes?

JOSEPH: I reckon I can help with their scratching.

LAWRENCE: Good for you, Grandfather!

GORDON: [*to* WALTER] You've got a mob of tender-hearted old women rapt and hanging off each word. Not me. [*To* ALL] They're no good! They've got to be sent on their way. We're letting him manipulate us.

Silently they take their seats. LAWRENCE *sneezes.*

GARY: What's happening? Why are we behaving like uninitiated men here?

ALBERT: Like fools.

JACOB: Why are we fighting each other? And not them?

GARY: Gordon, in particular, you disappoint me—

GORDON: Shut up. Fucking shut up.

GARY: You finished? … We need to take our duty seriously. We have nothing to gain or lose personally by our verdict. It's for the collective good that we make decisions.

JACOB: It's raining. The bark for my nowee will warp. And my new wife …

GARY: Shut up about your new wife!

JACOB: You still sore about that?

GARY: Well, we all know why *you* are so keen on battle, Jacob.

JOSEPH: What?

ALBERT: His new wife. She was promised to brother Gary. But brother Jacob—

JACOB: All's fair when you go to battle! When you win, you get the spoils.

ALBERT: Then we better be sure that *they* don't win. Ever.

No-one knows what to do.

LAWRENCE: Anyone want a lilly pilly?

GORDON: Come on!

WALTER: Yes, thank you, Lawrence.

LAWRENCE *throws a lilly pilly berry over.*

LAWRENCE: We should vote again, Mr Chair.

GORDON: Now you got the young fella running the show. You're hopeless, Gary.

GARY: Shut up!

Beat.

Let's vote—

ALL: Yes.

JACOB: Out in the open.

GORDON: Then we know everyone's position.

GARY: Any objections?

ALL: No.

GARY: Lawrence?

LAWRENCE: We allow them to land.

GARY: Gordon?

GORDON: Get rid of them. Forever.

GARY: Albert?

ALBERT: Shoo them away.

GARY: Jacob?

JACOB: Good riddance.

GARY: Grandfather?

JOSEPH: I'm okay to let them land. I want to help the poor things. And you, Gary?

GARY: Well …

ALBERT: You get everyone else to say their bit but we don't know what you think.

GARY: Okay. They are breaking the lore. But does that mean we should? Then they've won before even one spear has been thrown.

WALTER: That's what I was talking about. If we have always welcomed visitors, then we should now.

ALBERT: Whatever the consequences?

WALTER: I don't know what the consequences will be. Nor do you. But I know our lore. Our protocols.

ALBERT: Your vote then, brother?

GARY: I'm voting that we welcome them. As visitors to our shore.

LAWRENCE: He's flipped!

GARY: We don't even know if they will land. They could turn around by sunset and sail away. But if they land, we welcome them. Also, I'm being pragmatic. There are more of them than us. I don't want to start something we can't finish.

GORDON: That's the coward's way out!

ALBERT: Or good diplomacy?

GORDON: Unbelievable! There will be bad consequences! I tell you!

GARY: The vote is now: four to allow to land, three to repel.

GORDON *stands.*

GORDON: I'm signalling my mob right now. We will take up arms against them. There's no point talking anymore.

ALBERT: Wait! [*To* GORDON] What bad consequences? What you mean?

GORDON: What if they stay? Forever?

GARY *is exasperated.*

GARY: Visitors don't stay. That's why they're visitors. Walter?

WALTER: Of course they'll leave. Folk have come here on their nowees before. Coming, going, sometimes trading, but always leaving eventually. We have long memories, eh. We know their visits are a passing event, a fleeting encounter. We are still here and will be forever. Do you really think that just because they come ashore this one time that we might fade into nothingness, like smoke into the sky?

GORDON *gives him a slow clap.*

GORDON: Fancy words.

ALBERT: There's one difference with this lot.

WALTER: What?

ALBERT: There's more of them.

JOSEPH: How many now?

They look.

LAWRENCE: Ten …
JOSEPH: Ten …

▼ ▼ ▼

LAWRENCE: [*to* JOSEPH] Grandfather?
JOSEPH: Yes?
LAWRENCE: I feel an unusual sensation. So hot.
JOSEPH: But it's cool now.
GARY: Albert? Give us your thoughts. Your reasons.
ALBERT: There is one story that concerns me. From eighteen summers ago. A senior woman, she told me that a mob, the cloaked ones, had threatened the women and children, and tried to poison them.
GORDON: That's what I am saying! We are putting our women's lives at risk.
WALTER: Gordon, you speak of their violence. Often.
LAWRENCE: Maybe he's the violent one? Is that's what you're thinking?
ALBERT: You really have found your voice, haven't you, boy?
LAWRENCE: Have I?

But he's sick.

GARY: Everyone! Let Albert speak.
ALBERT: So, they snuck up on a group of women and children who were gathered to prepare an evening meal.

Faint echoes of an old English dirge and laughter.

The children were terrified. They were clinging to their mothers' breasts. Worse, the visitors had slaughtered two of the clan's totems, the black swan, and they flung them at the women's feet.[45]
WALTER: What did she do?
ALBERT: She said she couldn't do anything. She was a distance away, in a cave, attending to a woman who had just birthed.

▼ ▼ ▼

JOSEPH *squints at the sun.*

JOSEPH: What time of day is it?
GARY: The sun is almost set.

JOSEPH: You don't suppose we could come back tomorrow? There is a man I must cure.

ALBERT: [*to* JOSEPH] Grandfather—can't you see where the sun is in the sky?

JOSEPH: I'm old.

GORDON: Why are we talking about an old man's sight? This is an emergency.

GARY: [*under his breath*] Shut up already.

ALBERT: The woman who testified? She's as old as Grandfather here.

JACOB: Older.

ALBERT: Aunty could barely see …

JACOB: She mistook me for my cousin, and that was close up.

ALBERT: That's right. She was as old as the stars in the night sky.

WALTER: Perhaps what she saw wasn't a threat after all. Perhaps it was something else?

JOSEPH: Maybe a performance—that *bonjour* mob, they played at fighting with us. When my mob retreated and threw our spears at their feet as a warning, that lot laughed.

WALTER: Albert, are you still set in your opinion?

ALBERT: Of course I am!

Beat.

I'm vacillating.

LAWRENCE: What's that?

▼ ▼ ▼

GARY: Flip-flopping.

GORDON: They killed a totem!

WALTER: They don't know lore.

JOSEPH: They can learn.

GORDON: You don't know that.

WALTER: No. But given they left his country … [*pointing to* LAWRENCE] is there any real risk they will stay? Albert?

GARY: What's your decision?

ALBERT: At this moment, we can't *prove* they're a threat. We can't *prove* they'll stay more than three sunrises. So … I conclude that we should treat them with equanimity and grace. Welcome.

GORDON: Fuck that—

JOSEPH: Whoa—
GORDON: C'mon, men—we bring in our warriors. We go to war!
LAWRENCE: Whoa—

They all look at WALTER.

There's eleven …
GARY: And the vote is five to welcome them and two to repel—
WALTER: Actually—
GORDON: We should be spearing them!
GARY: We're stuck.
ALBERT: We're not going to agree.
JACOB: Look. It's his country—

He points at GORDON, *then at the others in turn.*

—not your country. Not your country. Not your country. Not your country. Not your country.[46] We should be behind him!
LAWRENCE: Grandfather …
JOSEPH: What is it, Lawrence?
LAWRENCE: Grandfather, can I lay down?
GARY: They have smaller nowees. A whole mob of them …
JACOB: I'm changing my vote.
GORDON: What? *What?!*
JACOB: You heard me. I'm over it. We've wasted too much time. All this yabba yabba. It's too late to do anything.
GARY: That's not a decision. That's putting your shield down.

LAWRENCE *lies down, sick. The others barely register.*

ALBERT: A minute ago you said you were sure about your vote. Now you have changed it—
GORDON: For *convenience's* sake? Or what? What kind of a man are you?
GARY: For once I agree with Gordon.
JACOB: Oi! Don't talk like that to me.
GARY: If you vote to repel them, do it because you are convinced that they are not worthy of our assistance. Or mean harm to us. If you believe they are worthy, or harmless, then vote that way. Don't be gutless.
JACOB: Watch it—
GARY: Do we send them away or allow them to land?

JACOB: Like I said. Land.
GARY: Give us your reason.
JACOB: Why should I?
GARY. We need to understand.

▼ ▼ ▼

JACOB: Maybe … maybe they're not completely wee-ree—bad. They might look hideous, they might be flawed. Guess what, so am I. But the main reason is—they are not going to stay. The pull of your own country is too strong. That's what I am gambling on.
LAWRENCE: Unc, I need to go home …
JACOB: I need to go home. I miss my country. They wanna go home too. This is not their country. They won't stay. I'm betting my life on it. Even the young fella here wants to go home. See?

LAWRENCE *nods weakly. And they register that he is unwell.* JOSEPH *kneels beside* LAWRENCE *and cools his forehead.*

GORDON: Jacob. Our alliance. Our mobs.
JACOB: That mob'll leave the day after next—like they did Bay mob's country—and we'll still have an alliance.
GARY: The vote is six to one. Only one vote to repel.
GORDON: You, lot are gullible! These people will betray us. We saw how they just kill someone for entertainment—with our own eyes! We've heard how they go out in groups of three or four and bang! someone is dead. That's how they are. Why can't you see it?
WALTER: Actually, I didn't vote in the last round.
JACOB: Of course you did.
GARY: You want to welcome them.
WALTER: Except the stakes are high … maybe they're very high.
JACOB: He's gunna change his mind! After all this!
LAWRENCE: He's vacillating?
JOSEPH: No!
ALBERT: No! You can't!
GARY: I agree! You made all the arguments. You said they could be taught. That they just didn't have the leadership.
JACOB: And that they have tools that might be useful.
JOSEPH: Though I still don't know what we would do with the extra time we save.

JACOB: And that they won't stay. They come, they go, those shiny ones.
GARY: Like a flash summer storm, over in no time.
JOSEPH: And you said we could cure them of any malady.
ALBERT: And that we needed to stick to our way of doing things.
WALTER: Mostly, you said those things. Not me.
ALBERT: But you were the one who turned us upside down in our thinking.
GARY: [*to* LAWRENCE] Lawrence, the one on the nowee, when you were up close, did he seem dangerous?

LAWRENCE *goes to speak, but coughs.* JOSEPH *bends down to listen.*

JOSEPH: He said they're harmless.
ALBERT: You encouraged us to talk, and what everyone said convinced the rest of us not to be afraid—
GORDON: I'm not afraid—
ALBERT: If we're not afraid, then there's no reason to repel them. And if we are not repelling them—
WALTER: I understand—I led you in a certain way.
ALBERT: —then we should welcome them.
WALTER: But we need to be sure. That what we are doing is *choosing*. Is this a choice we make?
GORDON: I'm not welcoming them. I'm not.

Now ALBERT *sneezes, violently.*

Sound of a big splash.

GARY: Look, look, a small nowee is in the water!

They look out to sea, panicking.

JOSEPH: We need to decide!
JACOB: I'm sick of this. I'm going home.

He stands up, but WALTER *gestures for him to sit. He does.*

ALBERT: We should let their women and children come ashore anyway.
GARY: And if he's not going to welcome them, who will? Grandfather?
GORDON: No! I forbid you! This is my country.
LAWRENCE: I'm not up to fighting …
GARY: Everyone agrees but you.
GORDON: You're not intimidating me! I'm entitled to my opinion!

They all watch him silently.

They're no good. There's not a one of 'em who's any good. They will hurt us. They will trample our land. They will poison us with their liquid. They will cut down our trees and muddy our water and take too many fish. They will hurt our beloved country.

If we get our warriors together … if we march down there now …

JOSEPH: You're all alone, brother.

Tense pause.

WALTER: Everyone has told their story but Gordon.

GARY: There's no time for stories!

WALTER: We have time.

JOSEPH *leaves* LAWRENCE*'s side and goes up to* GORDON *and pokes him in the chest.*

▼ ▼ ▼

JOSEPH: Gordon, what's going on? You're not telling us something. What is it?

GORDON *hangs his head.*

GORDON: I don't have words.

JOSEPH: Just try.

GORDON: The goorabeera. My father.

GARY: We've heard that story. We're going around in circles.

WALTER: Listen to him.

ALBERT *silently passes him the message stick.*

GORDON: I'm ten summers old. A kid with scabby knees. When the nowees arrive, the Elders choose my father to greet them. He's dignified. He marches down to the shore.

I'm so proud of him. I follow, hiding behind trees. He would have flogged me for disobeying him. He wanted me to be safe. But I wanted to see him welcome these aliens.

He steps towards them. He puts down his spear. Uncle Raymond is by his side. And the goorabeera rings out! Raymond flees. Coward!

And I put my hand on my mouth, to stop myself from crying out!

My father steps forward again, all alone. I am shaking. They are but one man's length away from him. He begins …

'This is my country.

My father's country.
My father's father's country.
I know its patterns, its season …'
Then the goorabeera rings out again.
And something strikes him.
Bleeding, he takes another steps towards them.
And they laugh. They mock him.
I see my father hurt.
I see the look of superiority in their eyes. Like they know they can defeat us.
Soon after they leave and he returns to the mob.
But within days my strong, brave father withers away. I sit with him.

GORDON *looks over at* JOSEPH, *who is caring for* LAWRENCE *in the same way.*

▼ ▼ ▼

GORDON: I tell him I had disobeyed him and suggest he flog me.
He's too weak. He dies.
And all I could do is throw stones … Stand behind a tree and throw stones like a little boy … I'm not that little boy now.

The men gather around GORDON, *comforting him as though the grief is raw. It is.*

JOSEPH: Gordon, you are grieving.
WALTER: Sorry business.
GARY: We all feel it.
GORDON: Fellas, if I was like a spear ready to fly … Don't take it personally, okay?
JOSEPH: Grief has fuelled your anger.
JACOB: Brother. We understand.
GARY: We're with you—
JOSEPH: Look. They are so close now I can see them.
ALBERT: Men. We know what to do. Call your clans in. Your warriors.

They all begin to whistle up their troops.

WALTER: We follow Gordon's plan. My men will come up over from the south.

JOSEPH: They are almost at the beach.

They adorn themselves with their kangaroo pelts. They step forward holding their spears, all except LAWRENCE.

ALBERT: Ready, men?
WALTER: Let's go.
GARY: Wait! Meeting adjourned.

▼ ▼ ▼

They step forward again, their spears are raised, ready to charge.

GORDON: Wait.
This is my country.
My sovereignty.
My responsibility.
I am my father's son. I finish what he began.

He puts down his spear. He steps forward.

[*Towards the boats*] This is my country.
My father's country.

I know its patterns, its seasons, its soils, the texture of them, the colours, the particular shade of green of the grass the patyegarang nibbles after a fire has swept through, at dusk, when the patyegarang is most hungry, and most likely to be speared.

I know its secret springs where a thirst can be quenched even in the driest season.

I know my country's smells. The exact scent of leaf litter where bulbs of the chocolate lily hide under moss, though it is not my job to collect them.

And where the hardest flint is to be found. For tools, for trading.

Its rivers are my blood, its rocky outcrops my bones, its winds are my breath as my lungs fill and empty. It is me.

When I welcome others, I honour my country.
We ask this, and this only.
While you walk on this country that you care for the land.
And that you look after the children of this land.
This is my country and my son's country.
In honour of my father, I welcome you to country.

ALL: Ngaya gawi niya
Gulya guwagu yana ngurra wu winjara njurra
Gay ngubaty gurung nula ngurra wu
Warra mi yana allowah.

GORDON *stands proudly. The other men stand behind him.*

THE END

Glossary of Aboriginal words

blue tongue - type of lizard
cuz - cousin (but not always by blood)
gadi - country (in the area around Sydney)
gammon - joking, pretend
goorabeera - musket
illalong - shield
jiliwa - toilet
lily pilly - fruit of lily pilly tree
mago - axe
mari - very big
maugro - fish
myall - stranger
nowee - boat
patyegarang - grey kangaroo
tidda - sister, girl
warra warra wai - go away
wee-ree - bad
wombah - crazy

Introduction to Annotations

The Visitors is a re-imagining, from my perspective as a First Nations woman, of the arrival of the First Fleet in 1788—the beginning of the colonisation of Australia by the English. Our knowledge of the events of 1788 is sourced from the letters, journals and books of the colonisers and explorers: Anglo (white) and men. In contrast, Aboriginal knowledge transfer—our history—was, and in many cases still is, an oral one and one that has not been preserved to the same degree.

What stories about the events of 1788 have failed, then, to be told? What perspectives have been overlooked or dismissed? Black American playwright Suzan Lori-Parks asserts that, when Black histories have not been recorded, it is up to Black playwrights to seek them out, and re-assemble the fragments into our own narratives:

> A play is a blueprint of an event: a way of creating and rewriting history through the medium of literature. Since history is a recorded or remembered event, theatre, for me, is the perfect place to 'make' history—that is, because so much of African-American history has been unrecorded, dismembered, washed out, one of my tasks as a playwright is to—through literature and the special strange relationship between theatre and real-life—locate the ancestral burial ground, dig for bones, find bones, hear the bones sing, write it down …[i]

In fleshing out this bricolage of a play, I scoured many journals, books and letters written by the early colonisers and explorers. Many historical facts are alluded to, or repurposed, throughout the script, some blatantly, and others more subtlety. In this publication of the play script I have annotated only a few. Mostly I have referenced first-hand accounts by (white, male) writers from the era, so that my 'version' of history cannot be easily dismissed. Less frequently, I have drawn on the research of contemporary historians. Either way, I have read between the lines—the subtext, if you like. Sometimes I have turned their withering gaze back on them, such as with Dampier's unflattering description of Aboriginal people, now directed towards the invaders.

Maori academic Linda Tuhiwai Smith posits that the creation of new Indigenous stories 'contribute to a collective story' that works to restore the place of Indigenous peoples:

> The story and the story teller both serve to connect the past with the future, one generation with the other, the land with the people and the people with the story.[ii]

I hope that is what I have been able to achieve with *The Visitors*. I believe that there is no exclusively 'white' history of Australia—when we—First Nations people—have always been here. There is no 'Black' history of Australia in the last 240-plus years, either. We are each other's shadows. To make sense of our shared history, we need to go back to the very beginning.

Jane Harrison

i Suzan-Lori Parks: *The America Play and Other Works*. New York: Theater Communications Group Inc. 1995.

ii Linda Tuhiwai Smith: *Decolonizing Methodologies Research and Indigenous Peoples*. University of Otago Press. 1999.

Annotations

1 "Several women appeared at a distance, but we could not prevail on the men to bring them near us." [Bradley 1802]

2 "I have frequently seen the men indulge at the expense of the weaker vessel, the women, who have been forced to sit in their canoe, exposed to the fervour of the mid-day sun, hour after hour … for without a sufficient quantity to make a meal for their tyrants, who were lying asleep at their ease, they would meet but a rude reception on their landing." [Collins 1798]

"Women line-fish from small canoes while the men fish with spears and usually on shore. Early colonists and later anthropologists agree that most of the food is gathered by women." [Karskens 2009 405–406]

3 "Love and war seemed his [Baneelon's] favourite pursuits …" [Tench 1793 in Flannery 1996 8]

"The procuring of food really seems to be but a secondary business with them [the men]; the management of the spear and the shield, dexterity in throwing the various clubs they have in use among them, agility in either attacking or defending … appearing to rank first among their concerns in life." [Collins 1798]

4 "The dialect spoken by the natives at Sydney not only differs entirely from that left us by Captain Cook of the people with whom he had intercourse … people living at the distance of only fifty or sixty miles should call the sun and moon by different names; such, however, was the fact. In an excursion to the banks of the Hawkesbury, accompanied by two Sydney natives, we first discovered this difference; but our companions conversed with the river natives without any apparent difficulty, each understanding or comprehending the other." [Collins 1798]

5 "… several parties of the natives, as they proceeded along the coast, who all greeted them in the same words, and in the same tone of vociferation, shouting every where 'Warra, warra, warra' words which, by the gestures that accompanied them, could not be interpreted into invitations to land, or expressions of welcome …" [Collins 1798]

6 "The canoe is made of the bark taken off a large tree of the length they want to make the canoe, which is gathered up at each end and secured by a lashing of strong vine which runs amongst the underbrush." [Bradley 1802]

7 "The laboratory and sick tents were erected, and, I am sorry to say, were soon filled with patients afflicted with the true camp dysentery and the scurvy. More pitiable objects were perhaps never seen." [White 1790]

8 "… they [Aboriginal men] laughed at and mocked the Europeans for their clumsiness and stupidity in the bush." [Flannery 1996 8]

9 "[After initiation] they were received into the class of men; were privileged to wield the spear and the club, and to oppose their persons in combat." [Collins 1798]

10 "The Sydney region people had established trade relations and routes between the coast and inland and beyond … News and ideas from distant places could arrive with lone messengers travelling through foreign country." [Karskens 2009 42]

11 "Many of their warriors, or distinguished men, we observed to be painted in stripes across the breast and back, which at some little distance appears not unlike our soldiers' cross belts." [White 1790]

12 "We put the boats onshore [in Botany Bay] near where we observed a group of the Natives … We then made signs that we wanted water, when they pointed round the point on which they stood … they directed us by pointing to a very fine stream of water." [King 1793 in Cobley 1962 19]

13 "… after receiving each a hatchet [of the use of which the eldest instantly and curiously showed his knowledge, by turning up his foot, and sharpening a piece of wood on the sole with the hatchet] took their leave …" [Collins 1798]

14 "… we fell in with a large party of natives … they were armed with spears and stone hatchets. One of the latter they very earnestly wished to exchange for one of ours." [White 1790]

15 "… many of the Trees, especially the Palms, were cut steps of about 3 or 4 feet asunder for the conveniency of Climbing them." [Cook 1768–1771]

16 "I advanced before them unarmed, presenting some beads and ribbands." [King 1793 in Flannery 1999 44]

17 "… [Lieutenant King] produced his handkerchief and tied it on one of the women 'where Eve did the Fig Leaf'; the natives then set up another very great shout." [Hughes 1987 85]

18 "… the gunner of the Supply [was] at some little distance, with a gun in his hand, an instrument of death, against which they entertain an insuperable aversion …" [White 1790]

19 "The report of the gun frightened them very much." [White 1790]

20 "... as soon as we aproachd the rocks two of the men came down upon them ... They calld to us very loud in a harsh sounding Language ... in all appearance resolvd to dispute our landing to the utmost tho they were but two and we 30 or 40 at least ... They remaind resolute so a musquet was fird over them, the Effect of which was that the Youngest of the two dropd a bundle of lances on the rock at the instant in which he heard the report; he however snatchd them up again and both renewd their threats and opposition. A Musquet loaded with small shot was now fird at the Eldest of the two who was about 40 yards from the boat; it struck him on the legs but he minded it very little so another was immediately fird at him ..." [Banks 1768–1771]

21 "[An Aboriginal man] stuck the end of his shield in the sand ... I fired a pistol ball through it. The explosion frightened him ... on my putting the pistol into my pocket he took up the shield, and appeared to be much surprised at finding it perforated." [White 1790]

22 "That Carstensz in 1623 and Governor Phillip more than 160 years later, should seek to establish a relationship with the people through kidnapping is evidence of the gulf in understanding between the races. It also indicates a callous disregard for the human rights of the inhabitants once these conflicted with the aims of Europeans.' [Willey 1979 19]

23 "The Governor's plan with respect to the natives was, if possible, to cultivate an acquaintance with them, without their having an idea of our great superiority over them ..." [Bradley in Cobley 1962 42]

24 "In the exercise of this weapon [spear] they are very expert. I have seen them strike with certainty at the distance of seventy measured yards. They are thrown with great force, and where they are barbed are very formidable instruments." [Collins 1798]

"... a spear was thrown at the people by some of the natives, who were lurking behind the trees and rocks. It was hurled with such force, that it flew a considerable way over the boat, although we were between thirty and forty yards from the shore." [White 1790]

25 "Some of these unhappy people [convicts] died after the ships came into the harbour, before they could be taken on shore—part of these had been thrown into the harbour ..." [Johnson 1790 in Flannery 1999 100]

26 "The inhabitants of this country are the miserablest people in the world ... who have no houses and skin garments, sheep, poultry, and fruits of the earth, ostrich eggs, etc ..." [Dampier 1697]

"... the inhabitants, too, are the most wretched and poorest creatures that I have ever seen in my age or time ..."
[Carstensz 1623 in Willey 1979 19]

27 "… they [Aboriginal people] had excellent teeth— unlike the white invaders." [Hughes 1987 14]

28 "They had not been landed more than an hour … but their came on the most violent storm of thunder, lightning and rain I ever saw. The lightening was incessant during the whole night and I never heard it rain faster." [Smyth 1787–1789 in Flannery 1999 60]

29 "… 6 small fires near the Shore, and mussels roasting upon them, and a few Oysters laying near … We tasted of their Cheer, and left them in return Strings of beads, etc …" [Cook 1768–1771]

30 "A quantity of Darts lay about the Hutts; these we took away with us." [Cook 1768–1771]

31 "The English picked up the Eora's weapons, left little piles of nails in return, and rowed away again." [Karskens 2009 35]

32 "We likewise presented them with a looking-glass, but this they received with indifference, and seemed to hold in no kind of estimation." [White 1790]

" … neither did they seem to admire anything that we had." [Dampier in Willey 1979 23]

33 "Fish enough was sometimes taken to supply about two hundred persons …" [Collins 1798]

34 Three sting-rays were taken this month, two of which weighed each about three hundred weight, and were distributed amongst the [settler] people." [Collins 1798]

35 "Stock: 1 Stallion 2 Bulls 19 Goats 5 Rabbits 35 Ducks 3 Mares 5 Cows 49 Hogs 18 Turkeys 122 Fowls 3 Colts 29 Sheep 25 Pigs 29 Geese 87 Chickens …" [Collins 1798]

36 "… one of the gentlemen with me sung some songs; and when he had done, the females in the canoes either sung one of their own songs, or imitated him, in which they succeeded beyond conception. Any thing spoken by us they most accurately recited …" [White 1790]

37 "… setting aside their human shape, they differ but little from brutes. they are tall, straight-bodied and thin, with small, long limbs. they have great heads, round foreheads, and great brows. Their eye-lids are always half closed, to keep the flies out of their yes, they being so troublesome here that no fanning will keep them from coming to one's face … so that, from their infancy, being thus annoyed with these insects, they do never open their eyes as other people do; and therefore they cannot see far, unless they hold up their heads as if they were looking at somewhat over them. They have great bottle-noses, pretty full lips and wide

mouths, the two fore-teeth of their upper jaw are wanting in all of them, men and women, old and young: neither have they any beards. They are long-visaged, and of a very unpleasing aspect, having no one graceful feature in their faces. Their hair is black, short, and curled, like that of the negroes; and not long and lank … the colour of their skins, both of their faces and the rest of their body, is coal black, like that of the negroes of guinea." [Dampier 1697]

38 "They wanted to know of what sex we were, which they explained by pointing to where it was distinguishable. As they took us for women, not having our beard grown …" [King in Cobley 1962 19]

39 "… The Iora respected their old men as repositories of tribal wisdom and religious knowledge, but the tribe would not hamper its mobility, essential for nomadic survival, by keeping the old and infirm alive after their teeth had gone and their joints had seized up." [Hughes 1987 17]

40 "As we sailed into the bay, [Botany] some of the natives were on the shore, looking with seeming attention at such large moving bodies coming amongst them. In the evening the boats were permitted to land on the north side, in order to get water and grass for the little stock we had remaining." [White 1790]

41 "… spirits they could never be brought to taste a second time." [Tench 1793 in Flannery 1996 54]

42 "Some of the natives came along-side the Sirius, and made signs to have their beards taken off. One of them patiently, and without fear or distrust, underwent the operation from the ship's barber, and seemed much delighted with it." [White 1790]

43 "… he [Frances Morgan] was hung there, exhibiting an object of much terror … to the natives his appearance was so frightful— his clothing shaking in the wind, and the creaking of his irons …" [Collins 1798 in Flannery 1999 148]

44 "From what I have said of the Natives of New Holland they may appear to some to be the most wretched People upon Earth; but in reality they are far more happier than we Europeans, being wholy unacquainted not only with the Superfluous, but with the necessary Conveniences so much sought after in Europe; they are happy in not knowing the use of them. They live in a Tranquility which is not disturbed by the Inequality of Condition. The earth and Sea of their own accord furnishes them with all things necessary for Life. They covet not Magnificient Houses, Household-stuff, etc.; they live in a Warm and fine Climate, and enjoy every wholesome Air … in short, they seem'd to set no Value upon

anything we gave them, nor would they ever part with anything of their own for any one Article we could offer them. This, in my opinion, Argues that they think themselves provided with all the necessarys of Life …" [Cook 1768-1771]

45 "[One of the Midshipmen] gave them a bird he had Shott, which they would not Touch; neither did they speak one word, but seem'd to be much frightned." [Cook 1768-1771]

46 "Gradually it dawned on the First Fleet officers that they had not encountered one people, but a constellation of peoples, each with their own country …" [Karskens 2009 37]

"… the 'principal business' of the settlers … was 'the clearing of Land, cutting, Grubbing and burning down Trees …'" [Bonyhady 2000 79]

"… one of the transports … attempted to land in one of the coves at the lower part of the harbour, but were prevented, and driven off with stones by the natives …" [Collins 1798]

References

Banks, Joseph. 1768–1771. *The Endeavour Journal of Sir Joseph Banks*. Project Gutenberg Australia. 2005. http://gutenberg.net.au/ebooks05/0501141h.html

Bonyhady, Tim. 2000. *The Colonial Earth*. Melbourne: Melbourne University Press.

Bradley, William. 1802. *William Bradley's Voyage to New South Wales*. Project Gutenberg Australia. 2019. http://gutenberg.net.au/ebooks19/1901251h.html

Cobley, John. 1962. *Sydney Cove 1788: The first year of the Settlement of Australia.* Great Britain: Hodder and Stoughton.

Collins, David. 1798. *An Account of the English Colony in New South Wales, Vol. 1.* Project Gutenberg Australia. 2004. https://www.gutenberg.org/files/12565/12565-h/12565-h.htm

Collins, David. 1802. *An Account of the English Colony in New South Wales, Vol. 2.* Project Gutenberg Australia. http://gutenberg.net.au/ebooks/e00011.html

Cook, James. 1768–1771. *Captain Cook's Journal First Voyage*. Project Gutenberg Australia. http://gutenberg.net.au/ebooks/e00043.html

Dampier, William. 1697. *A New Voyage round the World*. Project Gutenberg Australia. 2005. http://gutenberg.net.au/ebooks05/0500461h.html

Flannery, Tim. 1996. *Watkin Tench 1788*. Melbourne: Text Publishing.

Hughes, Robert. 1987. *The Fatal Shore*. London: Collins Harvill.

Karskens, Grace. 2009. *The Colony: A History of Early Sydney*. Crows Nest: Allen & Unwin.

White, John. 1790. *Journal of a Voyage to New South Wales*. London: J. Debrett.

Willey, Keith. 1979. *When the Sky Fell Down: The Destruction of the Tribes of the Sydney Region 1788-1850s*. Sydney: Collins.

www.ingramcontent.com/pod-product-compliance
Ingram Content Group UK Ltd.
Pitfield, Milton Keynes, MK11 3LW, UK
UKHW061133310726
14090UKWH00036B/917

9 781760 626761